How To Get Rich Sooner Than You Think!

Volume Two

by
Joanna Jordan

All rights reserved under International and Pan-American Copyright
Conventions. Published in the United States by New Start Publica-
tions, Inc., Sterling, Virginia
Copright © 1984 by Joanna Jordan

Editor Brenda Crawford

Library of Congress Cataloging In Publication Data
Jordan, Joanna

How To Get Rich Sooner Than You Think!
Volume 2
    I. Title.

ISBN 0-915451-04-2

Manufactured in the United States of America
9 8 7 6 5 4 3 2 1

TABLE OF CONTENTS

Chapter 16

Using Emotion Can Make You Rich

The advanced erudition of science has poked deeper and deeper into the field of psychology to find out why people behave as they do.

The findings of one branch of this scientific investigation have proved immensely valuable to those engaged in the everyday business of selling, where the scientific data is put to work earning money.

The knowledge that psychologists have gained about people serves the advertising and sales industry extremely well, enabling sellers to create and stimulate demand for new products and services by making people *want.* A working grasp of the basic psychological facts involved is indispensable in the conduct of a successful mail order business, since your success hinges entirely on how adept you are at making people want to buy what you have to sell.

Most of the things that psychologists have found out about people revolve around one central trait: They are, as individuals, *selfish.* (Not in the childish sense, but in the more general human sense.) This is not a criticism, but a demonstrably true aspect of the human species. All this means is that your individual prospect is wrapped up in her own desires, ambitions, and aspirations. In short, she is interested in herself. And you must become interested in her, too, if you hope to sell her anything.

People also are susceptible to things which appeal to their emotions. They will get thoroughly agitated or enthused about something of no consequence whatsoever, provided it is dressed in the proper emotional form. Emotion can get sales action like nothing else can, and the most effective sales copy always contains one or more strong emotional appeals.

How you build emotion into sales copy is a difficult process to describe. Perhaps the most practical way is to search other ads and sales letters for headlines and copy that are particularly moving to your own emotions, then adapt the methods used to your own copy.

The various forms that individual "selfishness" takes have been classified, and it is important for you to be aware of these when you set out to compose sales letters and ad copy for your product. There are twenty-three basic reasons why people spend their money, and here they are:

To make money	To escape pain
To save money	To be praised
To save time	To be popular
To avoid effort	To attract the opposite sex
To achieve comfort	To conserve possessions
To enjoy good health	To gratify curiosity
To protect family	To avoid criticism
To be in style	To realize individuality
To own beautiful things	To take advantage of
To satisfy appetites	opportunities
To emulate others	To avoid trouble
To be safe in making	To protect their reputation
purchases	

To sell anything to anybody anywhere, you *must* cater to one or more of these basic buying motives. This is as true in mail order as it is in personal selling...more so, because words-in-print are never as forceful as spoken words.

Fortunately, nearly every product you choose to handle will embody the satisfaction of one or more of the basic human wants, and your job will be to define those wants which a particular product satisfies, and then devise the selling phrases which connect a specific product feature with a specific buying motive.

Suppose you were selling a two-month course in bookkeeping. Do you think anyone really wants to be a bookkeeper? Probably not; it's refined drudgery, at best. But to sell your course, you don't attempt to sell a prospect on the idea, per se, of being a bookkeeper. Instead you sell her the idea that

2

she deserves a better-than-average income, a new car, a nice home, and the respect and envy of her less fortunate neighbors, and that a career in bookkeeping will help her get those things.

Take Cadillacs. Do people really buy Cadillacs because they transport the body from X place to Y place? A Ford will do that. Do they spend $29,000 because a Cadillac rides easier than an Oldsmobile? Few people have the educated posteriors to tell the difference. No, people buy Cadillacs to satisfy one of the more pronounced human wants, that of *prestige*. That's the only reason, though few Caddy owners would admit it openly. Owning a Cadillac (or a Mercedes or a Rolls-Royce) sets them above and apart from those who have to be satisfied with Fords and Chevrolets...gives them the means to publicly display their status and thus acquire prestige.

Take certain highly touted novels. Do people read them because they enjoy them? In many cases, no. They read them because the ads scare them into believing that if they don't read them, they will be cultural and social outcasts. Nobody wants to be thought of as a social clod, and a person will go to almost any length—even to ruining his eyesight in the process of reading boring novels—to avoid becoming one. This illustrates our motives "to be in style" and "to avoid criticism."

If you could examine a dozen mail order offers that have failed, you probably would find that one of the causes of their failure (in some instances the *only* cause) is that the sales copy fails to present the production terms of one or more of the basic human buying motives. Or, the copy will make a weak appeal to a less-important motive, completely ignoring several others of much greater importance to the prospective buyer.

A woman recently went to her advertising counselor with a line of simulated pearls and a sales letter she had written to sell them with. The letter had been mailed to hundreds of prospects without producing a single sale. On reading the letter, the counselor immediately saw that the copy began and ended with matters of little or no importance whatever as sales appeal: the type of plastic used in the pearls, the genuine

3

leather box they came in, the 8mm size of each pearl and so on. Not a line appeared anywhere in the letter that went directly to one of the basic wants.

The counselor suggested that he be allowed to rewrite the letter, which he did. Instead of physical details, he gave the prospect pesonal, selfish reasons for wanting to buy the pearls. Instead of telling her the pearls were made of Tenite plastic, he pictured the pearls on the neck of a beautiful woman that would add sizzle to the offer, and would be a smart addition to any lady's wardrobe. The new sales letter was tried and worked extremely well.

You can spend your time most profitably in studying people and what makes them tick. This knowledge is important in mail order, and it can be a fascinating study, indeed, especially when you remember that the things you learn are going to mean hundreds and thousands of dollars to you.

This study is made in all sorts of ways: by rereading the list of basic buying motives previously given; by observing people in stores and shops and asking yourself, "What is the real reason that person is making that particular purchase?"; by studying published ads and asking yourself which of the basic wants is being capitalized on, and by reading the sales letters you get in your daily mail to see how professional copywriters turn basic wants and motives into selling phrases.

Chapter 17

Testimonials: How to Get Them and How to Use Them

Nothing will help you more in selling products by mail than the consistent use of good testimonials. They are in a class with premiums and guarantees (about which I will have more to say later).

A testimonial will put teeth into your sales story for the simple reason that people may not believe what *you* have to say about your product in every case, but they will nearly always believe what a *satisfied user* has to say about it.

It is true that testimonials have been overworked in some areas of advertising and selling. People have come to be cynical and unimpressed by the use of testimonials from movie stars, famous tennis players, and other public figures in praise of automobiles, jeans, stock brokers and other products. But even these blatantly phony testimonials are partially effective.

Testimonials are especially valuable in selling a new product which has not been generally accepted by the public, or in selling an old product to a new market. In using testimonials, there are a few established rules to go by. One of these is that the testimonial must be *plausible,* or reasonable. It will defeat its purpose if it is so far-fetched—so exaggerated—as to sound trumped up or written by some kind of nut.

A firm selling a new lightweight cushion for the inside of your shoes steadily received testimonials from enthusiastic users of the product, but many of them were unusable in advertising because they were too implausible (even if, as in some cases, completely true). Some of the users would go so far as to say the cushion cured everything from back trouble to cancer...and may have believed their own words.

You can't use testimonials that cannot be proved to be true. Thus, even if a user of a patent medicine writes and says that the product cured him of this or that, such a letter cannot lawfully be used in advertising, unless his statement can be proved scientifically by authorities in the field. The law takes the position that an average user is not qualified to pass on the real qualities of a medicine or —only scientists can do this.

Whenever you use a testimonial, it has the legal status of your having made the same statements yourself. You can't print a testimonial in an ad, for example, and escape responsibility for its truthfulness by saying, "Well, that's what the user said in his letter."

Don't let the legal aspect of testimonials keep you from using them, however. Use testimonials in your sales material and in your ads, but be sure they are *plausible* and *true*, or at least provable.

Getting testimonials is not difficult if your product is a good one and fairly represented and sold. Some customers will, in fact, take it on themselves to write letters of testimony without your having to ask them to do so. But if you are in a hurry to get some testimonials and don't want to wait for the unsolicited ones to trickle in, you can do it by writing your customers and subtly asking them for a testimonial. There are different ways to go about this, but one good way is to compose a letter similar to the following and send it out to users of your product.

Dear Customer:

By now, you have had a chance to use [your product] and have made up your mind about whether it's all we say it is. If you feel that it is, we'd appreciate hearing from you... and will send you a little surprise gift for your trouble. If it isn't, won't you let us know anyway?

You see, a lot of folks want to use our product, but before buying, they'd like to hear what other users like yourself have to say about it. And we'd like to pass your opinion on to those future users, because we know your judgment and opinion will be respected.

You can help us convince these future users by letting us know, on the enclosed form, what you think of our product. Just write it in your own words, as you would tell it to a neighbor or friend. Our future customers will appreciate it just as much as we do.

Along with this letter you send a form (which can be printed) that provides space for the customer to write in his testimonial. At the top of this form you can put a statement like this: "I am _____, am not _____, more than happy with your [name of product] for the following reasons:"

Near the bottom of the form you provide a "release," worded in a manner similar to this: "This gives you permission to use the above statements in your advertising and sales literature. Date _____ Signed _____"

On receipt of the signed testimonial and release, you then send your customer an inexpensive gift, such as a ball-point pen, to show your gratitude and to establish consideration for the release.

In those instances where a testimonial comes in unsolicited, you should write the customer and obtain his permission to use his letter, asking him to sign a release form like that given above. Releases are necessary for photographs as well as written statements, and don't fail to get them in all cases before using testimonials in your ads and printed material.

Some of your customers will be glad to have you use their statements, but will prefer that their full names be withheld. So it is a good idea to provide spaces on your release form for the customer to indicate whether his full name or just his initials may be used.

In all cases, keep your original testimonial letters on file—preferably in a fireproof cabinet or safe. At some point along the way you may be asked by the postal authorities to produce the originals, and it can be embarrassing not to be able to do so.

Guarantee

Warranty

Chapter 18

Guarantees: A Must In Mail Order Selling

A good rule in mail order is this. *Never handle anything you can't guarantee.*

Stated backwards, it still makes sense: *Guarantee everything that you sell.*

A guarantee is one of the simplest, most powerful aids to mail selling you can employ. Yet the number of would-be mail order operators who stubbornly refuse to, or half-heartedly use a guarantee is appalling.

Guarantees should be used at all times, but they are especially important to the success of a new product and/or a new venture. When you arrive on the mail order scene with new products, you will be unknown, with no established record of fair dealing to convey your reliability and integrity. In this situation a strong, comprehensive guarantee on all your products can help pave the way to faster success.

Guarantees are of many types, but the most commonly used one is the basic "Satisfaction guaranteed or your money back." This guarantee is said to have originated in the nineteenth century with a man named Sears. . .who subsequently developed one of the world's largest enterprises, Sears, Roebuck and Co. It is also said, with a great deal of justification, that this simple guarantee was more responsible for the firm's huge success than any other single factor. It isn't hard to see why. For in those days a guarantee was unheard of. The rule of selling was "Let the buyer beware." Then along came a man who had the unprecedented courage to stand behind his products with the world's first blanket money-back guarantee.

The use of a guarantee never costs the operator a cent if she is selling a worthwhile product. Most people are honest in money matters and ask only that you send them what you say you will in your ads and sales literature. If you deceive them, they naturally have a right to—and usually will—squawk to the postal authorities. Of course, there are a certain number of professional gripers in the world who would not be happy with anything you sent them, but they are in the minority, and their existence is one of the occupational nuisances of the mail order business (or any other business, for that matter). You will inevitably run into some of these people as you go along, but if you know your product is good and are willing to stand behind your guarantee, you have nothing to fear.

While guarantees don't cost anything, except a little extra paperwork and postage every now and then, they can be highly instrumental in stimulating sales. Many more people will buy a guaranteed product over one that isn't. One mail order operator didn't quite believe this...although she believed in her product. Finally her advertising counselor prevailed upon her to put an iron-clad guarantee on her product, and sales went up nearly fifty percent. True, her refunds went up about five percent, but that represented a small price to pay for a very healthy increase in business.

Another good rule in mail selling is this: *Don't make any guarantee that you are not fully prepared to back up.* Nothing will get a customer so excited as welching on a guarantee.

Bear in mind that when you have to make a refund, said refund doesn't cost you the selling price of the product, it costs you only the shipping and postage involved, in most cases. If the product is returned undamaged, it can be resold.

Unusual guarantees are a way of putting originality into an otherwise staple or run-of-the-mill product. Nowadays, of course, the mass merchandisers have stumbled onto this truth about guarantees that mail order people have known for years. Many kinds of products are being guaranteed "for life," automobiles are being guaranteed "for five years," and so on.

A mail order guarantee should have a time limit of some kind on it, beyond which the customer cannot ask for a refund. This is to prevent her from sending the product back two or three years later, when she happens to need a few dollars, under the guise of being dissatisfied with it. Time limits are variable, depending on the product. Books, as a rule, are allowed fifteen to thirty days to be returned. Mechanical devices usually must be returned within ninety days. Highly durable goods might be returnable for as long as six months.

Don't fail to use guarantees in your business—individual products guarantees as well as a blanket company guarantee that covers everything you sell. Unusual and out-of-the-ordinary guarantees are good, too, and should be tried any time the product or situation warrants.

FREE!

Chapter 19

Premiums: Giving Your Customer A Free Gift Can Make You A Winner

Webster defines a premium as "an extra reward or recompense."

Salesmen, including mail sellers, call premiums the greatest device to stimulate sales ever conceived. And they're right.

Properly selected and used, a premium can put profit into an otherwise unprofitable one. It can sell things by mail that otherwise couldn't be sold at all through mail order channels.

No matter what you are now selling or plan to sell by mail, you can probably enhance its earning potentialities by judiciously choosing a premium to go along with it.

There came in the mail the other day a mailing piece from an outfit selling a very commonplace item; a travel bag. If you were to poll a dozen well-known mail order operators, they would no doubt be unanimous in stating that such a staple product, available everywhere at low cost, could not profitably be sold by mail. But this particular firm is doing it successfully, and they are doing it on the strength of a powerful premium offer.

The major TV Mail Order companies *(pots, pans, cookware and knives)* could not thrive as they do except by going all-out for premium offers. A Los Angeles jewelry firm could not have built a list of over a million customers throughout the United States without the continued use of premiums. A lot of successful newcomers to mail order would not be successful without an understanding and skillful use of premiums.

Many moribund merchandisers, of course, fail to see the handwriting on the wall and stubbornly refuse to use premiums. "I'd rather go broke than give something away free" is their attitude. And that occasionally is what happens.

13

You are not, as you can see, actually giving something away free. You are making use of a premium to force the sale of another item, in which there is enough profit to make the total transaction a satisfying one to everybody concerned.

In using premiums to stimulate the sale of *your* product, you must remember that a premium has to be free...with no strings attached. This doesn't mean that you can hike the price of your product up enough to cover the cost of the premium; not in very many cases, anyway. The premium must be something over and above the product, and its costs must usually be absorbed out of your normal product profit margin.

You may object that such a practice will increase your selling costs. True. But it is also true that your gross sales will increase (often tremendously), resulting perhaps in more cost of each product but definitely in more total sales and net profit on over-all operations. Suppose, for example, that you can normally sell fifty orders of a given product at an average price of $29, without the use of premiums. Suppose further that you can throw in a premium that costs you four dollars and drive your gross sales up to a hundred orders at an average of $29. Would it be worth doing?

There is a popular delusion among some mail order, beginners and old pros alike, that it is better to take a *large* profit on a *few* sales than a lower profit on a much bigger volume of sales. This delusion has nipped many promising businesses in the bud. The real smart cookies in business these days don't try to make all their money on one customer. They realize it's better to make a ten percent net profit of $500,000 worth of business than it is to make forty percent on $50,000 worth.

A premium must not only be free, but it must *have value in itself*. It must be something that your typical prospect would like to possess. Something that is entertaining, instructive, informative, utilitarian, or a combination of those.

A premium should be related to the product you're selling, but in no case should it satisfy the desire for the main offer. That is, your premium should not parallel the use or appeal of your main offer to the degree that if your customer owns the premium, she has less reason to own the main product. On the contrary, a good premium is one that whets the appetite for the main offer.

14

One of the easiest ways for a mail order firm to develop a premium program is to start issuing free certificates with the purchase of items, each certificate entitling the buyer to a discount on future purchases. This not only stimulates initial sales but results in additional business. It is possibly the widest used of all premium plans in mail order and is adaptable to any product or service. Suppose you are selling a line of cook books. To the purchaser of your advertised cook book you send along a printed certificate giving her a specific discount when she buys some of the other books in your line. In fact, this certificate can be worth up to fifty percent of the amount, as she paid for the first book causing her to come back for several more cook books or publications on related subjects.

A lot of mail order companies are making the offer more enticing by inserting clearly in their ads and sales letters that the customer will get the free gift or premium when she orders the main proposition, but the premium is hers to keep *FREE* even though she should choose to send the product back for a refund. This works very well, not only in stimulating sales but in promoting confidence in your firm.

In all forms of mail order the purpose of a premium is not only to get your prospect to order but to order *quickly*. So it is a good idea, when offering a premium, to put a time limit on it. That is, an order must be received within a certain period of time, or before such-and-such a date, in order to entitle the customer to the free gift.

For a premium to be effective, it frequently isn't enough that it be something of value. You may have to give the premium itself a good sales pitch in order to create a desire for it. Even though it has value, and is free, you must work hard at making your prospect want it. In fact, many direct-mail offers devote more sales effort to generating a desire for the free premium than they do to trying to sell the product itself...on the sound theory that if you can make the premium sound good enough, the prospect will buy the main offer almost sight unseen in order to get the premium.

Use premiums whenever and wherever you can. But always be sure they are free, have value, and are worth acquiring.

Chapter 20

Your Mailing List Is The *"Life-Blood"* Of Your Business

If you plan to sell by direct mail, it is not enough to have a superb product and a wonderful sales letter. You must, in addition, have the names and addresses of the people who are logical prospects for your product. And you must have enough of these names that you can continue to send out your mailings without running out of prospects.

Fortunately, getting an adequate supply of names is no longer a problem for most firms, provided it is definitely known what type of prospect is needed. Before you set out in search of a thousand or a million prospects' names, you have to first decide the kind of prospect you want, and this—obviously—is determined by what you are selling.

Should you be selling a book on how to make money, then your best prospects would be people who have bought money-making books from other firms. Should you decide to sell a line of kitchen goods, you could get the names of known mail order kitchen goods buyers.

The business of supplying name-and-address lists has kept pace with the growth of the mail order business and is in itself a large segment of the industry. As you know, or will learn, there are several large firms (for the most part located in New York and Los Angeles) whose business is to supply you with names and addresses of many different classes of mail order prospects, in virtually any quantity. The names of these mailing-list houses can easily be gotten by subscribing to the mailing list directory from S.R.D.S. or by subscribing to the mail trade journals, such as *DM NEWS,* or *Direct Marketing,* where you will see their various ads.

Whether you plan to rent name lists in the immediate future or not, it will pay you to write one or more of the prominent list houses and request their catalog. It won't cost you anything, but it will give you an understanding of the list business and how it can serve your own future needs.

The accuracy of any given mailing list will not usually be greater than ninety-five percent, although most legitimate list sources make intensive efforts to keep their lists "clean," removing inactive names and correcting addresses. In planning your mailing, make allowance in your costs for the approximately five percent of your letters that will be undeliverable.

Names cost money, of course. Whether you compile them yourself or rent them from a mailing-list broker, they will cost you anywhere from $55 to $70 per thousand. In setting up your schedule of selling costs, be sure to allow for the cost of the names. You will also have to pay for getting the names put on your envelopes by your printer/mailing house. (In dealing with a list broker, you normally have an option as to whether you want the names on pressure sensitive labels, mag. tape, or cheshire labels.)

Most reliable list brokers offer a free consultation service, which is quite valuable if you are not sure what type of prospects you should mail to. If you are in doubt, write your list broker or source explaining what you have to sell and including specimens of your sales literature. They will, in most cases, be able to suggest the best lists for you to use.

If you plan to sell exclusively from space ads in magazines or newspaper, then you won't have a list problem. You will, after a while, be able to compile a list of your own customers and inquirers, which you can then turn around and rent or sell to other mail order firms. This provides you with an additional source of revenue and profit. For this reason, it will pay you to set your names up on a computer that keeps them in alphabetical and zip code order.

Chapter 21

What Does Dept. PS-785 Tell You?

Before describing some of the innumerable ways to key your ads, perhaps we should first discuss the why of keying ads. If you have never run any display or classified ads in newspapers or magazines, the reason for keying, or coding, may be somewhat obscure to you.

Let's approach it this way. Suppose you were selling a certain product by mail, and you decide to put the same ad in two different magazines at the same time. Suppose also that you had had no prior experience with either of these two magazines, but you had heard that they were both good "pullers." If you ran the same ad in both magazines simultaneously, once the orders started coming in, how would you know which magazine pulled which order?

You wouldn't, unless the ads were keyed. The reason you want to know which magazine pulled which orders is so you can get some clear idea of which is the best magazine to use in the future. If the two magazines containing your ad pulled two thousand orders in the aggregate, and the ads were not keyed, you would have no way of knowing how many orders to attribute to each magazine.

Conceivably, out of the two thousand orders, one magazine might have pulled seventeen hundred orders and the other magazine only three hundred orders. (There can be that much difference between magazines having ostensibly the same circulation and type of readership.) Naturally, if this occurred, you would not want to spend any more money on the magazine that pulled only three hundred orders.

The foregoing is a simplified illustration, but the lesson is clear. The process of keying ads can be valuable not only in telling which publications pull the best, but in other ways as well. Some companies, for instance, will run not just one but two or three ads in the same magazine at the same time, on the same product, to determine the effect of position. And when you are running the same ad month after month, keying it will eventually tell you what the seasonal characteristics of the magazine are; i.e., which months produce the most orders per dollar spent.

The mechanics of keying an ad are as varied as you want them to be. One way is to change your mailing address slightly from one ad to another, and one publication to another. Mail order buyers always address their orders exactly as your address appears in the ad, and there is little danger of their omitting the key when it is part of your address. If the ad shows your address to be "57 E. 40th St.," you can key it the next time by changing it to read "57 East 40th St.," and the next by making it read "57 East 40th Street." Or you can throw in a letter of the alphabet (provided it won't confuse your postman) like this: "57-A E. 40th St."

Another way to key ads is to include a department number. For one ad you can use "Dept. A," for another, "Dept. B." Some firms expedite matters by using the magazine's initials in the department key: An ad in *Better Homes & Gardens* would thus be keyed "Dept. BH-1." The department number, of course, appears in addition to your regular address.

If you use a post office box, you can easily key the box number. For instance, if your box number is 139, you can make it read "P. O. Box 139-A" in one ad, "P. O. Box 139-B" in the next, and "P. O. Box 139-C" in the third.

If your ads include a coupon, you can key them in any of the ways described, or be content with the built-in key which coupons automatically contain. That is, the reverse side of the coupon will tell you which issue of a magazine it appeared in, since ads are shifted around from one spot to another from one issue to the next, and the back side of your coupon will have portions of ads and editorial matter from that particular issue.

Direct mail is also easily keyed. It can be done by putting a symbol or letter of the alphabet on the return envelope or order form. Or you can simply change the color of order forms and envelopes from one mailing to the next.

In regard to keying, it is a good idea to work up a chart showing all the keys you are using and post this in your office or shipping room so it can be referred to as the orders come in.

Also, it is good practice to show on your order forms and customer computer files just where each order originated, and its date of receipt. Later on this can be of value in making long-range appraisals of mailings and media.

The best key I've found to use is the one that describes the month, year and name of publication that you used to advertise your product; *Dept. PS-785* means: Popular Science, July issue, 1985

Printer

Printers and Printing: Can Make Your Small Company Look Like A Major Mail Order Firm

Perhaps nothing is so important in mail order as *good printing.* You can compromise and hedge on the other tools of your business, but you dare not do so on your printing.

That's because the only contact you have with your customer is through printing. If your printing is superior, she is more inclined to believe that you and your product are superior. If your printing is shoddy, she may feel the opposite.

As every mail order counselor and operator knows, even a bad piece of copy will usually produce some orders if it is handsomely printed on quality paper. But the best copy in the world will fall flat if it is poorly printed on cheap-quality stock.

In setting up your mail venture, there are a few printing essentials you must have at once to get off to a good start. These will require a modest outlay of capital, but as you'll discover later on, they are more than worth it.

For one thing, you'll need a quantity of letterheads. Although you may plan to sell directly from magazine ads, involving no sales letters, catalogs, or reply envelopes, you will still need letterheads on which to correspond with sources of supply, answer complaints, and answer special requests.

You don't have to buy a great quantity of letterheads in the beginning, but those you buy should be of good quality, well printed on a good grade of bond paper. They don't have to be flashily done up in two or three colors; you can get by with a simple black-and-white job if the type styles and layout are carefully selected and arranged. The minimum quantity of letterheads you can economically buy is five hundred to a thousand. (The same is true of nearly any other kind of printing.) This quantity of letterheads, in one or two colors on fifty-pound white bond paper, will cost you anywhere from $100 to $200, depending on the printer.

The Stationery House does outstanding work. Send for their free catalog. 1000 Florida Avenue, Hagerstown, Maryland 21740

Letterheads call for matching envelopes, and you will need a similar quantity of these, from the same printer. Shipping labels also will be required, but you can usually get by at the start by purchasing stock labels at the office-supply store. Later on, when your volume of business justifies it, you can have your own labels printed at a cost of about $10.50 per thousand.

Some beginners attempt to get by with a rubber stamp to save the cost of printing letterheads and envelopes. A rubber stamp has its value in the mail order business (for endorsing checks, etc.) but should never be used in the place of good printing. Its use immediately marks the user as an amateur.

The subject of printing brings up the subject of printers. Whether you like it or not—and it can get to be a chore—you have to deal with printers. Many of them are downright incompetent; a number of them know their trade but for some reason or other don't always pass their skill along to their customers in the form of good printing; and of course, a lot of them are reputable businessmen who will try hard to give you a fair price on a decent printing job.

The difference in quality of work among different printers is often vast indeed. The same is true of their prices. In time you will be able to locate and use a printer who combines the happy medium of quality, price, and service, but if you make a few mistakes in judgment in the beginning, you won't be unusual.

In general, when dealing with printers, always get a written estimate or quotation on a printing job before you place the order. Make sure that such quotation specifies the type of paper that is going to be used, and obtain samples of the paper when you get the quotation.

Don't confuse stationery printers with mass mail order printers. They are in most cases two different companies.

In dealing with mass mail order printers always follow the rules given below:

Once you have a quotation from one printer, take your job specifications to another printer and get another estimate or quotation. (*Don't* show the second printer the quotation you got from the first.) After enough estimates have been acquired in this manner, you can then make up your own mind as to which printer is the one to use.

It is also a good idea to make the printer show you samples of work he has done for others, of a kind similar to yours. This is particularly important when you are buying a job that involves photographs (or halftones, as they are called), a job using more than one color of ink, or a job where there is to be a lot of solid-ink coverage. Printers differ widely on these points, owing to the differences in presses used.

Chapter 23

Mail Order Questions and Answers

What Fields of Business Present the Best Mail Order Opportunities Today?

This is difficult to answer. However, there appears to be room for, and a need for, new mail order businesses in the specialty frozen seafoods, women's fashions, jewelry, men's high-quality electronic devices, specialty gift items, weight-loss equipment, publishing *cooking and health,* health foods and products, diet aids, and women's ready—to—wear sportsware of all kinds. There is a continuing need for good information in the income opportunity and self-help book field. And, of course, there is always opportunity in the consumer-goods field, selling everything from greeting cards for Christmas to computer specialties for business owners to household and garden items for homeowners.

Is It Necessary To Have a Completely Original Idea or Product To Succeed in Mail Order?

Definitely not. Many so-called original mail order ideas are merely adaptations or switches on old ideas. Most successful mail order ideas consist of 1) finding a fresh way of selling an old product; 2) introducing a standard product into a brand-new market by discovering new uses for it; 3) reviving a product which has faded from public view, but which has a strong appeal to a new generation of buyers; 4) modifying an obsolete product to fit a modern market.

How Many Mail Order Businesses Are There in The United States?

Figures vary, but best estimates set the number at or near twenty thousand.

What Is the Future for a Small Mail Order Business?

Practically unlimited for a well-managed one offering good products or services at fair prices. The country is growing at an astounding rate, and this fact means opportunity for growth and expansion at a similar rate.

What Is the Average Yearly Profit of the Twenty Thousand Mail Order Businesses Now Operating?

Only *Maxwell Sroge's book "Inside The Leading Mail Order Houses"* can tell you that. The average is probably somewhere around $85,000. But this can be misleading, because many small operations make little or nothing, while others show annual net profits of $11,000,000 or more. The amount depends almost entirely on the skill and abilities of the individual operator.

Maxwell Sroge Publishing, Inc., 731 N. Cascade St., Colorado Springs, Colorado 80903

Why Are So Many People Interested in Mail Order...and Why Do So Few Actually Wind Up with Their Own Businesses?

Because there are more wishful thinkers than there are doers. It is one thing to be interested in making money, but quite another to do something about it. Why are there so many employ*ees,* and so few employ*ers*? Why are some folks content to spend their lives driving trucks and punching time clocks? It is not a lack of opportunity that prevents these people from having businesses of their own, but rather a lack of initiative, desire, ability, or sufficient motivation.

How Many People Actually Buy by Mail?

Literally millions. For instance, in 1983, one million four hundred thousand people bought seeds and plants from the Michigan Bulb Company by mail; over three hundred thousand bought imported reproduction prints and Christmas cards from the Metropolitan Museum of Art; nearly half a million bought household decorative items from the Joan Cook Mail Order Company; over three-quarters of a million people bought weight-reducing equipment, calculators and high-quality luxury electronic items from the Sharper Image earning Richard Thalheimer a record $90 million dollars; nearly four hundred thousand ordered toys from the Highlights for Children catalog; over two hundred and fifty thousand people ordered an income opportunity book from a Washington, D.C. publishing firm; and so on, ad infinitum. These are just a few random examples to give you an idea of the range and scope of mail order. There are thousands more, but these are sufficient to establish the fact that mail order is truly big business.

What Kind of Product Is a Beginner Most Likely To Be Successful With?

Those products she knows best and likes to handle most.

How Many Products Should a Beginner Start With?

Except in unusual cases, not more than one or two. But she should be prepared to add to these by staying on the lookout for potentially good sellers.

What Is the Federal Government's Attitude Toward Mail Order?

The Federal Government favors and encourages the development of legitimate mail enterprises. It is good for the economy, good for small business, and contrary to popular opinion, good for the efficient operation of the Post Office Department.

Is It a Good Idea To Borrow Money To Finance a Mail Business?

No. Mail order has a high element of chance in it, and there's no such thing as a *sure* thing...neither in mail order nor in any other phase of business. Borrowed money might be used to purchase equipment and other items that have lasting value, but don't use it to finance an ad or direct-mail campaign until long after such campaigns have already been proved successful.

If a Person Owns a Small Retail Store, Should She Sell it To Go into Mail Order?

Definitely not, unless the store is operating at a loss, in which case she will want to sell it, anyway. A retail store can be instrumental in the success of a mail order enterprise, because it means you already have established wholesale sources, space to work in, and possibly a good line of credit. Many operators have found the combination of retailing and mail order to be an ideal way to build a volume of business. Owning a store can help offset the dull mail order seasons by providing you with a flow of local business, and vice versa. Mail selling techniques can often be adapted at the local level to increase the amount of retail business a store produces.

Is a Rural Resident Under a Handicap in Mail Order Work?

Living on a farm or in a small town is no handicap in mail order, with the possible exception of making it difficult to get your mail rapidly.

How Much Better Is a New York or Chicago Address Than a Small-Town Address?

Practicaly none, except for some specialized products, such as business publications and technical services. The general trend is away from the city, except for certain occupational groups. A small-town address is just as good as a big-city address. The important thing is not the address but the person behind the address. Some of the nation's most successful mail businesses are located in small towns.

Is It True That Anything Can Be Sold by Mail?

No...not *as is*. But nearly anything can be sold by mail provided it is given the right twist in price, guarantee, premium, or terms of sale. Relatively few staple products can be sold by mail without first giving them some unusual twist.

What Is the Surest "Sure Thing" in Mail Order?

The class of products that comes nearest to being a "sure thing" in mail order is that which embraces the self-help and income opportunity field; i.e., books, manuals, and newsletters. Although this class of products doesn't always represent the biggest mailing list potential, it usually does offer the greatest safety.

Is There a Magic Formula or a "Big Secret" to Mail Order?

Yes. And some of the big mail order companies will be glad to take you through their plants, let you study their literature and talk with their personnel...learn everything about their business, in fact. They are completely secure in doing this because they realize that the only "big secret" in mail order is hard work, determination, sound management, and imagination...more or less in that order. Any of the several good books on the subject of mail order will tell you all the "secrets" there are. The rest is up to you.

Is It True That a Single Small Ad Often Will Pull a Fortune?

Most of the time, no. But, there have been— and will continue to be—very rare instances in which an advertiser pulls a large amount of business from one insertion of one ad. One such case reports a man in Virginia that spent $7,000 for a full-page magazine ad and received nearly $57,000 worth of orders. Another is a woman in Vermont who is said to have pulled close to $500,000 dollars worth of business from one full-page ad in a national Sunday magazine. But these are exceptions, not the rule. It takes even a good ad several insertions, in different publications, to pull its maximum number of orders, and the ad must be repeated steadily if it is to continue to pull.

Is There Any Scientific Way To Take the Gamble out of Mail Order?

No. The success of a mail order venture—like show biz—is dependent solely on the reactions of the public to your offer, and the public does not often lend itself to the precise manipulations of a slide rule, except in psychological terms. Dealing with the public is an art, not a science. Science does play its part in mail order, however, particularly the science of statistics, which is used to measure and check the effectiveness of direct-mail or ad pull. But science won't *get* the orders for you; it can only tell you whether you got them at a profit and whether you should repeat or extend a given promotional effort.

Is It True That a Mail Order Business Can Be Expanded to Great Size Just by Running More Ads in More Magazines?

Yes, provided your ad has been proved not just once but several times to be a steady puller, and provided further that you can find enough good magazines to run it in. For example, one firm ran a two-inch ad in one magazine for two months, pulling a total of $5,000 worth of business for an ad cost of about $1,500. A second magazine of the same general type was added, and it too pulled an aggregate of $5,000 in orders for approximately the same ad cost. Other magazines were gradually tested and added until the company was grossing over $100,000 a year. This feature of building a business simply by increasing the number of ads run is one of the most attractive aspects of mail order. In following such a plan, you must be careful, making sure at each step of the way that the magazines pull a profitable number of orders for each dollar spent. This is a matter of testing.

Should a Beginner Employ an Advertising Agency?

The advice and counsel of an experienced ad agency can be extremely valuable to a beginner. However, there are only a handful of legitimate ad agencies who cater to the mail order trade (or have any thorough-going mail order experience themselves), and they won't usually handle a newcomer unless she is prepared to spend anywhere from $2,000 or more per month for ad space. Normally, a legitimate agency's services do not cost you anything, except for specific items of copy and artwork they are required to do for you. Its compensation is derived from the cost of the advertising space you use, based on fifteen percent of the amount you spend. This is paid to the agency by the publisher, not by you. Only recognized agencies are allowed this commission, and the space costs you, the advertiser, the same amount whether you place your ad through an agency or direct. Since the amount an agency earns on a small ad is fairly low, you can see that it cannot afford to give you very much time and attention for so little compensation.

However, I suggest you open your own in-house *recognized* advertising agency and save the fifteen percent commission. John Chriswell's book entitled: "$25,000 Dollars For A Few Hours Work Doesn't Seem Fair!" has a whole section devoted to this subject.

Write John Chriswell, P.O. Box 139, Sterling, Virginia 22170. The price is $10.

Should a Beginner Work at Home or Rent an Office?

Work at home, by all means, unless you already occupy an office or store and can handle your mail business there. One of the nice things about mail order is that it doesn't make much difference where you set up shop...in the corner of a bedroom, in the garage, or in the attic. You don't meet your customers face-to-face, so you don't have to put on any front. If you have the space, work at home until you see whether your project is going over or not. Doing this will help conserve your capital.

How Much Equipment Should a New Operation Have To Start With?

The less money you tie up in equipment at the start, the better off you'll be. However, there are certain indispensable items that you must have to conduct your business in a businesslike way. You'll need a small postal scale, for one thing, to weigh your outgoing packages and letters. You'll need a typewriter, though this can be rented in the beginning. You'll need a small 3" × 5" card file, with cards on which to keep your customer records. You'll need shelves and racks to hold your stock and mailing materials, but these can be fashioned out of spare lumber or crates. Your correspondence will call for a place to file carbon copies of letters, as well as original order letters and inquiries. These files can be crates or heavy corrugated boxes partitioned to accommodate the letters and orders. You'll also need a small desk, a typing table, and possibly a large table to be used for packing and shipping purposes. In addition, you may need a tape dispenser (plus several rolls of tape), and several hundred mailing bags or boxs. Incidentals include a stamp dispenser, letter opener, rubber stamp for endorsing checks and money orders, dating stamp, paper clips, and rubber bands.

A good source for some of these supplies are: The Freund Box & Can Company, 185 W. 84th Street, Chicago, Ill. 60620, The W.A. Charnstrom Co. *Mailroom Equipment Catalog* 9801 James Circle, Minneapolis, MN 55431. Ask for free catalogs from both.

Should a Beginner Attempt To Issue a Catalog?

No. A catalog is probably the best all-round mail selling tool. The problem it presents to the beginner, however, is the selection of a wide range of items to go into it (and arranging for a multitude of supply sources), as well as the high initial cost of preparing and printing the catalog. The average beginner would be wise to try one or more single products in the beginning, and as good sellers are found, keep adding to them until a *line* of products is being handled. When you have such a line, then it becomes feasible to put all of your products, at least 176, into catalog form and promote the catalog through ads and direct mail.

I'm Not A Beginner. How Elaborate Should a Catalog Be?

A catalog can be any size and length, from a brief four-page folder listing just a few products to the fifty-page job issued by such giants as Sharper Image. A catalog can be printed in black and white on ordinary paper and still be effective, but full color illustrations on glossy stock obviously will be even more so. Catalogs as a whole do a good selling job because they are not thrown away as other types of literature are. Compiling a catalog requires special art-and-copy know-how (not to mention special merchandising know-how), and it is wise to enlist the aid of experienced professionals when undertaking a project of this kind.

What About the Companies Who Offer To Supply Ready-Made Catalogs with Individual Imprints?

There are a number of companies around, in the gift and housewares field, which will provide you with preprinted mail order catalogs illustrating several dozen to several hundred products. These catalogs have no company name on them. You place your order for a quantity of them (usually a thousand or more) and *your* name is imprinted in the appropriate space. The cost of these catalogs varies, but usually is on the order of $100 per thousand. You are supposed to buy the catalogs, mail them out to your prospects, and then relay the orders received to the wholesale company. You receive a commission on each sale, ranging from twenty-five to fifty percent. This allegedly puts you in the mail order business, with no inventory to carry or any expenditure other than the cost of the catalogs, mailing list, and postage. The trouble with deals of this kind is that usually the catalogs are poorly produced or are filled with a lot of merchandising lemons that won't sell enough to cover your costs. A number of the companies operating the syndicated catalog idea are not interested in selling merchandise at all, but make their money selling high-priced printing. They prepare the catalogs in huge quantities at low cost, then dole them out to a multitude of small mailers a thousand or more at a time, at a large profit to themselves. Aside from that, the principal disadvantage of preprinted catalogs is that the same customers receive several copies of the same catalog, but all bearing different company names and addresses, and this makes the whole operation ludicrous. There are a couple of exceptions to the foregoing, of course, where the firm preparing the catalogs in the first place makes an honest effort to produce a catalog that will actually pull a profitable number of orders. *Most are multi-level mail order dealers.* Such catalogs are prepared by mail order firms who have already been successful in consumer selling, and compile their catalogs around their proven sellers. Such catalogs can be used at a profit if you already have a list of *customers* who have bought something from you through magazine ads or direct mail. It is not advisable to send a quantity of these catalogs out to "cold" mailing lists; doing so will rarely ever produce a profit.

What Is the Mortality Rate Among New Mail Order Companies?

No exact data is available on this, but it is said that about fifty percent of all new mail ventures fail within the first year, and only about twenty-five percent manage to survive the first two or three years.

What Are the Major Causes of Failure?

Some fail through lack of capital or proper management. But most fail through lack of mail order know-how, lack of willingness to take the right chance at the right time, lack of attention to the important details of the business, lack of a good product "sense," and similar reasons.

Is It True That People Throw Letters Away Without Reading Them?

Yes, but they never throw one away without first knowing what it's about. Some otherwise astute merchandisers won't use direct mail, in the erroneous belief that their letters will be thrown in the wastebasket unopened. If this were true, half the direct-mail outfits in the country would be out of business. The fact of the matter is that any sales letter will get enough attention to show the prospect what it is about. No one, not even the biggest business executive, is going to throw a letter away without first determining whether it contains something new and useful to him. It is this fact that proves the importance of a good "opener" in a sales letter. The opener (as well as the "teaser" on the outside of the envelope) usually decides the fate of the mailing piece... whether it goes sailing into "File 13" or goes back on the desk for a more careful reading.

How Do You Go About Finding New Products?

Staying on the alert for new products to sell by mail is one of the most important functions of a successful mail order operator. There is no specific way to go about this. In general, it is accomplished by keeping your eyes and ears open and lining up good current information sources. You can watch your state and local newspapers for reports of new items produced in your neighborhood or region. You can scan the merchandise sections of national papers such as the *New York Times* and the *Wall Street Journal.* It helps to buy samples or subscriptions to trade journals in the fields that interest you. Watch the mail trade magazines. Set up an idea file, and whenever you see a likely-looking item file it away for future consideration. When you think of an original idea that has possibilities, write it down in outline form and put it in your file. Observe products being sold by your competitors and others in mail order. Attend the periodic trade shows that are held in major distribution areas of the United States.

Can Postcards Be Used To Sell by Direct Mail?

Only in a very limited way. There is no record of a major mail order success being built around the postcard as its prime advertising format. (Adaptations and elaborations of the postcard—such as large self-mailers—are, of course, a staple of the direct-mail business.) The postcard does have its use, however, especially for acknowledging inquiries and orders, because it is inexpensive and travels via first-class mail.

What Kind of Products Are Not Suited to Mail Selling?

Elsewhere in this book I have given a list of the positive qualities of a good mail seller. These qualities can be stated in reverse to determine what *isn't* likely to be a good mail seller. A product is not usually suited to mail selling if it carries a profit margin of less than forty percent, and even that may be too small a margin. A product is not suited to mail order unless you have a steady source of supply for it. It is not suited to mail order if it complicated and requires elaborate explanation and instruction for its satisfactory use. Products that sell for over $400 are not ordinarily good mail order products (although there are outstanding exceptions to this rule, as there are to the others given). Items which are sold widely in retail stores are not good mail order products unless they are given some unusual sales twist. Nor are items which do not open the door to a future repeat sale to the same customer, either of the same product or a similar product.

Chapter 24

What You Should Know About the Post Office

All mailing pieces that originate in the United States for delivery to destinations within the United States fall into one of four general classes: First Class, Second Class, Third Class, or Fourth Class.

First Class mail is probably the class most familiar to you if you have not had previous mail order experience. Into this class falls personal letters, postcards, business-reply envelopes and cards, and other types of mail which you may elect to send first class by paying first-class postage.

Second Class mail is a class set up to accommodate publishers of newspapers, magazines, and other periodicals that qualify. This allows them to enjoy fast distribution of their issues at a very nominal cost.

Third Class Bulk mail is the catch-all for business mail and everything that doesn't go by one of the other classes. The main purpose of the third-class provision is to give mass mailers an economical means by which large quantities of purely sales material can be distributed. As a mail order operator you will be more concerned with this class than any other.

A letter that travels third class gets to its destination in about seven to fourteen days (except during the big rush seasons, such as Christmas), but costs about one-half as much to mail. If you are on anyone's mailing list, particularly as a mail order buyer, you no doubt are deluged with sales letters from many other mail order companies wanting you to buy something from them, also. The majority of the letters you receive of this kind will have been mailed third class. This class also includes catalogs, circulars, pamphlets, broadsides, self-mailers. . . .

41

There are several identifying marks of a third-class letter. For one thing, it must be so identified somewhere on the outside of the piece. It will usually have printed indicia rather than a postage stamp, said indicia showing the third-class permit number, city, and state. Some mailers decorate these indicia or otherwise dress them up to the point where they appear at casual glance to be official postage stamps and cancellations.

Third-class mail also includes bulk-rate mailing privileges that are especially valuable to those firms who mail many thousands or millions of pieces per year. While you can get a permit to mail third class free of charge, you must pay an annual fee of $80 in order to enjoy the bulk-rate privileges. (To use the printed indicia, rather than precancelled stamps or postage metering, you must also pay an additional $40 fee.)

To qualify as bulk mail the letters must be mailed no fewer than two hundred at a time, and they must all be identical in size. In addition, they must be sorted by state and city and zip code, with a minimum of ten pieces for each town or city, and must be tied in bundles prior to delivery to the post office. To the big mailer this sorting and tying (normally a post office function) is a small price to pay a mailing house for the excellent savings made in postage.

Of course, in the beginning you may not be ready or willing to go in for heavy bulk mailing. You may have only a few hundred or a thousand letters to mail. Without paying any special fees, mail them at the first-class rate. It is not necessary to sort your letters by city and state when mailing in this manner.

Fourth Class is also an important class to the mail order businesswoman. This is another term for what is called book rate. If you know what book rate is, you know what fourth-class mail is. All books, cassette tapes, and instruction video recordings can be mailed book rate.

Mailing your product packages by the U.S. post office or by UPS, you will notice that the postage is governed not only by the weight of the parcel but also by the distance it has to travel. The farther it goes, the more it costs. (This isn't true of first class letters.) The Post Office Department and UPS have set up a standard scale of distances known as postal zones, and the United States is divided into eight of these zones. The zone in which you are located is your local zone, and packages mailed within your community get the local-zone rate. Zones 1 and 2 include everything within a 150-mile radius of your location, and the rest of the zones comprise ever-widening radii of distances from you. Zone 8, for instance, includes those places that are 2,800 miles or more from you; Zone 4, those that are 400 to 700 miles away.

This business of zones may be confusing to you until you have begun to mail packages out. After you have mailed a few orders, though, you'll have it pictured clearly in your mind. In case you want to determine the amount of postage your packages require, before you take them to the post office, or have UPS pick them up, drop by your local post office or UPS headquarters and pick up a zone-and-postage chart. Most postal scales have a built-in zone scale which automatically tells you how much postage is required provided you know the distance from mailing point to destination. Most office-supply stores and all post offices have ready-made distance-and-zone charts that will simplify the task for you.

A *business-reply permit* is one of the most useful things in mail order, whether you are selling by direct mail, catalog, or inquiry follow-up. As you already know, to get the maximum number of orders from your mailing pieces, you must make it easy for your customer to order. One way you do this is by enclosing a business-reply envelope for your customer to return her order in.

A business-reply permit number is yours for $40. You merely fill out a brief form, and when it is approved (a matter of a few days), you are assigned a number. You then take this number to your printer and have him print a supply of business-reply envelopes (or cards, if that is what you prefer). These envelopes and/or cards have to be printed to conform to a prescribed appearance and size, but most printers have standing forms to go by and need only your permit number, name, and address to do the job properly.

When a business-reply envelope comes back to you from a customer, it will come postage due and cost you twenty-seven to thirty-five cents; depending on the weight. However, since every envelope that comes back contains an order, you will find that you don't mind paying the premium. And by using the business-reply form, you'll also find that you receive more orders than you would otherwise.

While most of your customers will send cash, check, or money order, a small percentage of them will ask you to send their order C.O.D. You don't need to be told that this stands for "collect on delivery" and that the postman on the other end of the line collects from your customer, then sends you a money order for the amount involved. There's nothing to shipping C.O.D. except that it takes a little more time than regular shipments. And it costs an extra handling fee, over and above the postage, which you may pass along to your customer.

The only difference is in the way in which you get your money.

The mechanics of shipping C.O.D. are simple. The post office will provide you with C.O.D. tags and show you how to fill them out. You merely attach a tag to each C.O.D. package and present it at the parcel post window. The post office will do the rest. You do, as you'll learn, have to pay the parcel post and C.O.D. fees in advance, when you mail the package. But you can be reimbursed for these by adding them to the amount the post office collects from your customer.

My advice is to forget C.O.D.

A P.O. Box is a handy thing to have in the mail order business, if for no other reason than that it permits you to get your mail on Sundays and holidays. (There's no suspense like having to wait an extra day or two to get your mail when you're in the mail order business.) A box doesn't cost much, and anyone is entitled to one provided it is to be used for a legitimate purpose. In some cities, however, there are more people wanting boxes than there are boxes to go around, and in such an event you usually have to put your name on a waiting list.

Boxes are rented on a semiannual or annual basis. And the rental fee is payable in advance. (There's no credit at the post office.) The use of a box has its disadvantages, especially for a new, unknown mail order form. Prospective buyers hesitate to send money to a firm using only a post office box number. After you become better established and acquire a reliable name, the use of a box will not affect your business to any appreciable degree.

Your post office offers many other services besides those described here—such things as money orders, insurance, special delivery, air mail, stamped envelopes and overnight delivery. Remember, the post office is there to help you and serve you. Don't hesitate about going to it when you have any kind of question or problem. When you're not sure whether a piece should be mailed third class, fourth class, or first class, take a sample of it to your postmaster and he will tell you how to mail it. This applies to any other postal matters that come up. If your local post office can't answer a specific question, they will get the answer for you from Washington. When in doubt, always ask the people at the post office. They'll help you out, and it won't cost a penny.

Chapter 25

What You Should Know About Copyrights

As you may have observed, and as we have stated before, the easiest, safest, quickest way to build up a paying mail order business is to sell something which you create yourself or someone creates for you.

The reason is this: When you sell your own product, you have complete control over its distribution. No one can buy it except from you. You have no competitors in that exact product. The entire nation is your market.

You don't have to be a marketing expert to realize that it is better to have the whole cake to yourself than to have to slice it up among a dozen or a dozen dozen competitors. When you handle your own offering, over which you have exclusive control, you do not have to divide the cake with anybody.

There are several ways to get control of a product that has such priceless exclusiveness. One is to design and manufacture (or have manufactured to your specifications) some unique device, gadget, or other consumer product of a tangible nature. But this method involves long, drawn-out patent searches and applications, expensive tooling and manufacturing, and costly promotion. All of which is O.K. if you have the time and money to devote to it.

Another way to get a product that no one can sell but you—and no one can buy except from you—is through the written word. And when you sell the written word, your exclusive control over your product is assured by *copyright*.

It is no accident that there are probably more firms selling books, courses, and manuals than any other single class of mail order goods. The reason they do is simply that only through copyrighted publications can they achieve originality and exclusiveness of product cheaply and with little risk.

Thus, if you want to take the short route to getting an exclusive product, do it through writing...and copyright what you have written. You don't have to be a creative writer or even a journalist. If you have an idea for a course of instruction, a self-help manual, a money-making book...jot down the things you know in orderly, readable form, print the work, copyright it, and sell it.

This is rather a long prelude to the subject of copyrights, but the purpose of approaching the matter in this oblique fashion is to impress upon you the value of copyrights in the mail order business and to encourage you to take advantage of them. If you already have something to sell—if you're not interested in selling the written word—then, of course, you probably will not have read this far.

Copyright covers a multitude of creative and non-creative sins. Such things as dramatic compositions, songs, works of art, and photographs all come within the domain of copyright. We are concerned here with only one classification, however, and that one is labelled "books."

In the language of the copyright office *book* means just about anything committed to paper and reproduced by mechanical process. A book can be a catalog, a booklet, a leaflet, a pamphlet, a brochure, and so on. But to the copyright office it is still a book. For all practical purposes, the term "book" covers just about everything you will encounter in the mail order business.

The procedure for getting yourself a copyright is as follows:

1) Write to the Register of Copyrights, Library of Congress, Washington, D.C. 20005, and request the proper forms and instructions for copyrighting a book.

Bear in mind that you print your work with the copyright notice on it before you file for a copyright. You cannot copyright anything before it is published.

The final step in copyrighting is:

As soon as your "book" comes off the press, take two of the best copies and send them, along with the proper fee and the copyright application forms, to Copyright Office, Library of Congress, Washington, D.C. 20005.

A copyright is yours to do with as you see fit. You can publish and sell the work yourself or you can grant someone else the privilege of publishing and selling what you have written, in exchange for a flat fee or a royalty based on the selling price. Since a copyright represents a valuable piece of property, it can be willed to heirs, who can exploit it as they see fit.

When you assign or sell the rights to a work in which you have copyright, the agreement must be in writing, and it must be recorded in the Copyright Office within three months.

The word "published" as used in the above context is a general term covering all conventional reproduction processes. It does not mean that your work has to be printed on a printing press and bound with a leatherette cover. Instead, it can be produced by any of the economical processes, such as home typewriter, duplicator copier, and offset, and still be considered as having been published. No fancy covers are needed. In fact, you don't need any covers at all. The first page can serve as the cover, if necessary.

You can get a comprehensive outline of the copyright law by sending two dollars to the Register of Copyrights, Library of Congress, Washington, D.C. 20005.

Chapter 26

Some Do's and Don'ts for Mail Order Operators

Do give your company a name which fits the nature of your operation without implying nonexistent facilities or inordinate size.

Do use your own personal name in your firm name when an assumed name would sound ostentatious and unreal.

Do visit your county clerk when you start doing business, whether you use just your own name or an assumed name. In either case, it is wise to register the name with the county clerk, and in some states this registration is required by law.

Don't fail to investigate the laws of your state regarding the sale of particular items. While there is no federal license required to do business by mail, some states require certain licenses and put a tax on certain classes of goods. Your local tax assessor can help you in these matters or at least refer you to the people who can.

Don't begin selling taxable items, such as cigarettes, unless you've determined how much tax is required and whether it is to be paid to the state or federal governments. In most instances you will be acting as a dealer, and your supplier can apprise you of the tax situation regarding a particular product. Generally, such taxes are passed along to the consumer, although you may have to keep account of them and make periodic remittances to the government.

Don't risk your reputation and mail order career by handling an item of questionable nature or value. There are too many good things around to sell without your having to handle any product that cannot be ethically sold.

Do guarantee your products and stick with the guarantee. A good guarantee can build a business rapidly; a guarantee that is not honored will drive customers away, and create ill-will.

51

Don't say anything, or allow anything to be said, in your ads and sales literature that is not the truth. On the contrary, more sales will result when you deal in facts and present them sincerely. This does not preclude, of course, a certain amount of "romance," or putting the facts in the best possible light.

Do stand ready to go to any reasonable length to placate an unhappy customer. Return her money, replace her merchandise, apologize for the misunderstanding—but under no circumstances get hot under the collar and write her a stinging letter telling her what an unreasonable _____ she is for complaining about your products. Your biggest stock-in-trade is goodwill and the continued patronage of satisfied customers.

Don't get involved in any "trust schemes," whereby you send your products out to people who did not order them, with a request that they keep them and pay for them. While sending goods out on trust is not illegal, it nevertheless is frowned upon by the postal authorities. If a product is not good enough to be sold competitively, then you have no right to unload it on a trust basis.

Don't manipulate the prices of your products to make it appear that the customer is getting a price reduction when she actually is not. If you say that an item previously sold for $15.95 and is now going for $7.50, be absolutely sure that such is the case.

Don't state that a diet preparation is a "cure" for anything. In making claims for diets, you are on very dangerous ground. You can't make any claims that cannot be substantiated by proof... and *you* have to do the proving. In selling any product to be used in the treatment of the human anatomy, you must know exactly what you are doing. Nor does it relieve you of responsibility to be merely acting as agent for another manufacturer or distributor.

Do remember these rules when labelling a formula or preparation that you intend to market:

1) Information that appears on the label must also appear on the package or be legible through it.

2) All information on the label must be easily seen and not obscured by pictures or other matter.

3) All information required on the label must be printed in English, though a foreign language may be used in addition to English provided the same information appears in that foreign language.

4) The label itself must give the name and address of the manufacturer, or distributor; must tell the quantity of the preparation in the package; must describe and state quantity of habit-forming drugs if such are contained; must give the common or usual name of the drug; must give adequate directions for use; must provide warnings against unsafe use by children; must warn against excessive amounts and lengths of time; must indicate limits of therapeutic value.

Chapter 27

Your Mail Order Business Organization

There are three general types of business organizations or ownership: *sole proprietorship, partnership,* and *corporation.*

If you are planning to finance your business yourself, run it yourself, and take all the profits yourself, then you will own the business yourself, and this type of ownership is known as "sole proprietorship." This is the commonest form of business organization, and most small mail order businesses fall into this category.

There are several advantages to being a sole proprietor. For one thing, you are not obligated to take advice from or share managerial duties with a partner. You make all the decisions yourself without having to consult anyone, unless you wish to. At year's end if there is any profit, it all belongs to you. Also, as a sole owner you are not faced with the complications which arise from the legal technicalities of a partnership or corporation. In most states the law does not require you to file any formal documents when you are doing business as a sole proprietor. You simply register your name with the county clerk and start doing business.

There are a couple of disadvantages, however, to running a business with only yourself as owner. One of these is that you are limited in the amount of capital you can raise to put into it. There is no partner to call upon when you need extra capital, and since you are not a corporation, you can't float a new issue of stock to raise more money.

In a sole proprietorship you as an individual are wholly responsible for all of the company, and this can affect not only your business credit but your personal credit as well. In a partnership the debts are assumed on a proportionate basis between or among the various partners.

While most mail order businesses of modest size require a fair amount of capital, they don't always necessitate taking in a partner. About the best reason for entering into a partnership is to have someone around who can share the work and assist in managing the business, as well as someone who can contribute additional skills and ideas. Ideal partnerships are often worked out between partners who have complementary skills; for instance, a person who knows production might profitably team up with someone who knows advertising and sales.

If you do form a partnership with one or more people to carry on a mail order business, you will be wise to get the terms of the partnership down in writing. This takes the form of a *Partnership Agreement,* and the only sure way to get such a form executed properly is to have it prepared by a lawyer. You can, in some cases, get by with a simple oral agreement between yourself and your partners. But unless you know them extremely well, it is best not to rely on oral agreements; because if the business founders and sinks, there would be no room for disputes as to who is going to pay what.

A corporation is a business form very much like a partnership, except that the partners are known as *shareholders,* and they are not liable for the failure or success of the corporation, or any of its obligations. In the eyes of the law a corporation is an entity in itself, and the human beings involved in the operation of it are merely the implements that are used to make it function.

To organize a corporation, you must hire a lawyer and file the proper forms with your state government. In most states the Secretary of State is the agent who handles corporation matters. Once having made application the state grants you a *charter* under which you are allowed to issue and sell stock for the purpose of raising capital needed to start and operate the business.

Corporations are unwieldly for the most part, from the viewpoint of the average mail order operator, and it is a good idea to postpone any incorporation plans you may have until you get the business off the ground. After it has become successful, it is an easy matter to incorporate if it should appear advantageous to do so.

Chapter 28

The Perfect Mail Order Product

The *perfect* mail order product probably does not exist. But if you should ever run across one, in all likelihood it will possess the characteristics listed below. Any such list, of course, is subject to many successful exceptions, but nevertheless, it is a guide worth knowing and using when you are making a product search.

The Perfect Mail Order Product
— is not sold in retail stores at all, or to only a limited degree.
— is one which sells for twenty-one hundred percent times what you have to pay for it.
— is one which is in demand by a fairly large segment of the over-all population.
— is one which is readily understood by the prospect, without necessitating lengthy instruction or education in its use.
— is one which sells in the $15 to $29 price range.
— is one which generates a demand for more of the same product or creates a desire for additional products of similar kind.
— is one which doesn't go out of style, doesn't deteriorate, doesn't spoil while in storage.
— is one over which you have exclusive production and/or distribution control.
— is one which has some distinctive, exclusive, or unique feature about it to set it apart from competitive items of a similar kind.

— is one which can be packed and shipped in readily available packing materials, with a minimum amount of damage in shipment.
— is one that can be mailed or shipped for a postage cost not more than ten percent of its selling price.
— is one that can be backed with a strong guarantee without resulting in excessive returns.

don't sell these!

Chapter 29

Getting in Touch with Suppliers

Getting yourself established with sources of supply (manufacturers, wholesalers, etc.) is a relatively simple matter provided you observe certain rules of good business practice. In many cases you will be dealing with relatively large firms, and it is apparent that such firms do not wish to get involved with amateurs, hobbyists, or others who appear to have no chance of becoming good, steady dealers.

Most manufacturers and distributors are anxious to do business with you, however, if your correspondence with them indicates that you know what you are doing and show promise of developing into a consistent buyer of their goods. As a matter of fact, you will be better off not attempting to buy wholesale at all until you have definitely made up your mind that you are going into business and intend to handle a certain class of goods. If you are already established as a retail dealer, of course, then these points will offer nothing new to you.

The first requirement, perhaps the only indispensable requirement, of a new mail order business is a businesslike letterhead. Such a letterhead should tell 1) who you are; 2) where you are; 3) the nature of your business; 4) your telephone number; 5) your correct mailing address. A few dollars spent on having a professional-looking letterhead prepared for you will decidedly pay off in the long run. To begin corresponding with prospective suppliers without such a letterhead marks you as an amateur or an individual who is trying to "get it wholesale" for his own personal use. In either case, you are not likely to get much response.

The second important rule in getting established with suppliers is this. Always *type* your letters neatly, accurately, and in a prescribed letter form. This may sound trite, but you'd be surprised how much weight an attractively typed letter carries with the people on the other end of the line, especially if you have never met them or had any personal contact with them in the past.

The third rule is: Get to the point quickly. Don't beat around the bush. State exactly what you want, whether it's a catalog, price list, or just information. These people are busy and are more likely to respond quickly to a letter that is brief, to the point, and specific.

The fourth rule is: Make it easy for them to reply. If they are known to charge two dollars for their catalog, then send the money along with your first letter. In writing for information about a specific product, or for information of any kind, enclose a stamped, addressed reply envelope.

The fifth rule is: Keep a carbon copy of all correspondence with suppliers. This will eliminate any possibility of future disputes or misunderstandings.

Two specimen letters are supplied here. One of them is for use in requesting general information; the other, for use in locating a supplier of a particular item. You can use the letters as is or modify them to fit a special situation. At any rate, they are yours to use, and they have been proven to be effective in accomplishing their purpose.

Specimen Letter A

To be used when making original mail contact with a pro-spective supplier. Letter can be changed to fit any similar situation. Type on your own letterhead.

Date

Name of Supplier
Address
City, State, Zip Code

Dear Sir/Madam:

We wish to offer our retail mail order customers new prod-ucts, of merit and value, that are in good supply.

It is our understanding that you have one or more items that are well suited to our program, and we are writing to request a catalog or descriptive literature on your line, as well as a schedule of dealer discounts and delivery information.

Since we sell through mail order channels, we naturally cannot take on new items indiscriminately, because our products must measure up to a set of mail order standards of price, appeal, weight, and so forth. However, the items we do select have a potential for enjoying a large volume of sales, and for this reason we can give you reasonable assurance that substantial purchases will be made from time to time.

Until such time as satisfactory credit arrangements can be made with you, all purchases will be made on a cash-with-order basis.

Thank you for an early reply.

Yours very truly,

Your Name

Specimen Letter B

To be used when you wish to find a supplier of a particular item. Type on your letterhead.

Date

Name of Firm
Address
City, State, Zip Code

Dear Sir/Madam:

We are trying to establish a source of supply for (name of item, description, etc.), and it is our understanding that you may be able to supply us with this product from your regular stock.

On receipt of information from you, and contingent upon suitable discounts and delivery schedules, we shall be glad to place an initial order.

Should you not be able to supply this item, we would greatly appreciate your referring us to another possible supplier.

Thank you for your prompt attention.

Yours very truly,

Your name

Chapter 30

Mail Order Record Keeping

Like any other business, mail order requires accurate, systematic record keeping. This includes day-to-day and month-to-month sales and expense records, as well as the added detail of listing keyed orders and inquiries, and recording direct-mail test results.

The basic purposes of a good record-keeping program are 1) to tell you whether you are making or losing money, and how much; and 2) to make it easy to file your income tax returns when the time comes. Also, there will be times when you will want to tally up your real worth, your "net" worth, for the purpose of establishing bank credit or an enhanced credit rating.

Mail order records don't have to be elaborate; the main thing is to keep *some* kind of record of every transaction made, in such a manner that at a later date you can run totals and get a quick picture of what has been taking place in the business.

For a small fee a public accountant can help you set up a simple system that you can maintain yourself, or if you can afford it, you can—at a small monthly rate—have him do the work for you.

An alternative is to buy a stock bookkeeping system (the Ideal systems are excellent) from your office-supply store, selecting the one that best serves your particular needs. Such systems are made for many different kinds of businesses and are available for $8.50 to $12.50 each.

If you want to keep your system as simple and uncomplicated as possible, here is a suggestion. Buy a conventional three-ring loose-leaf binder and a quantity of blank white sheets to fit it.

You then divide your book into four sections (identifying each section with a file tab). Section 1 is "Record of Orders Received"; Section 2 is "Record of Sales"; Section 3 is "Record of Purchases"; and Section 4 is "Record of Expenses."

All you need do then is take a ruler and pen or pencil and rule the sheets in each section into vertical columns and horizontal lines spaced wide enough apart to accommodate the items of information that are to go into the respective spaces.

Section 1, "Record of Orders Received," should have eight columns on each page. These columns should be headed, from left to right, as follows: Date Order Received; Name of Customer; Address; Amount Enclosed; How Remitted; Date Order Filled; Amount of Postage; Remarks.

Section 2, "Record of Sales," is ruled off in the same way, but has only five columns and headings: Date; Quantity; Amount; Description of Items; Remarks.

Section 3, "Record of Purchases," has eight column headings: Date Ordered; Received; Supplier; Item; Quantity; Unit Cost; Total Cost; Remarks.

The last section, "Record of Expenses," also has eight columns: Date; Description; Postage; Advertising; Printing; Office Help; Professional Service; Other Expenses. Make the "Other Expenses" column a wide one, since it is a catch-all for many miscellaneous expenses such as insurance, rent, and utilities.

With such a homemade record system faithfully kept and kept current, plus your bank deposit slips and statements, you can at any given time produce an accurate profit-and-loss, or financial, statement—at least until the business has grown to a point at which you need a full-time bookkeeper.

In this connection, it goes without saying that you should open a bank account in your company name right at the start, and any time a purchase is made—or bill is paid—do it by company check. Good bank records are as important as your other records, and a cancelled check is indisputable proof that a certain expense has been incurred and covered.

Chapter 31

A Check List of Mail Order Costs and Expenses

At the start of your mail order career it is easy to overlook or ignore a number of costs and expenses which must be included in your records if a true picture of your operation is to be gained.

For example, the cost of your product is more than the unit cost you pay the manufacturer or wholesaler for it. Here are the cost factors that go into the total amount you pay for a product:

1) The basic unit amount paid the manufacturer or wholesaler

2) Allowance for those units damaged in shipment, replacement of unsatisfactory units to customers, refusal of 40 percent of C.O.D. units by customers, in-house deterioration and breakage, etc.

3) Cost of additional assembly work in your plant if same is required

4) Shipping charges to your plant or office from the supplier

5) Postage or shipping charges to your customer

6) Cost of packing and wrapping materials and labor

7) Storage costs

Aside from product cost there are a variety of overhead expenses which you will incur, and which should be recorded in your record books. Among your overhead items will be these:

1) Rent

2) Salaries to employees

3) Salary to yourself and partners

4) Utilities
   a. Electricity
   b. Automobile or truck
   c. Telephone
6) Office supplies
7) Taxes
8) Insurance
9) Licenses if required
10) Accounting or other professional services

Your third big category of expenses is advertising. Over and above the cost of the amount of newspaper or magazine space you use, there will be these added costs:
1) Printing
2) Copywriting
3) Photographs and/or artwork
4) Typesetting
5) Photostats
6) Copyrighting service
7) Ad agency service
8) Mailing lists
9) Addressing, folding, stuffing
10) Postage

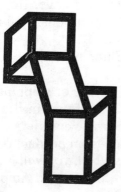

Chapter 32

A Step-by-Step Guide To Your First Million Dollar Year

The following is a reliable guide to operating a mail order business, with each point given in the briefest possible terms. This will also serve as a refresher course in everything that has gone before, and is supplied in this form for quick reference and periodic study.

1) Choose an unpretentious, easy-to-remember firm name.

2) Try to convey an air of informality and friendliness in your literature and advertising.

3) Use a street address for your mailing address in preference to a post office box if possible.

4) Select a product that has consumer appeal and is well made.

5) Try to select a product that fills a definite need.

6) Select a product that is not widely sold in stores.

7) Select a product that has something unusual about it.

8) Sell a product over which you have exclusive manufacturing or distribution control if possible.

9) Sell a product that leads to a repeat sale or an auxiliary sale.

10) Steer clear of attempts at manufacturing in the beginning if it is avoidable. (Better to farm out the manufacturing in small quantities than to incur expensive die and tooling costs.)

11) Choose items that have a strong element of "newness" about them in preference to items that have been repeatedly sold by others.

12) As you can, add additional items until you have a line; it is hard to make much money from one product.

13) After one item has proved to be a good seller, look around for a second item to start advertising, then a third, and so forth.

14) If there are personal services that go hand-in-hand with your product, offer them also.

15) If the product lends itself to sampling, by all means offer a small sample of it to your prospects for a modest price, with credit for the cost of the sample to be applied to a larger order.

16) Choose products that are light in weight (less than twenty pounds after packing), so that they may be mailed cheaply.

17) Avoid having to buy custom-designed cartons and other packaging materials; handle items that can be shipped in stock containers available from your supplier.

18) Figure postage costs into your selling price if possible.

19) Make all shipments prepaid, NO C.O.D.'s.

20) Use a neatly printed shipping label that is large enough to accommodate all necessary information.

21) Address shipping labels by typewriter, not by hand.

22) Use labels that have "Return Postage Guaranteed" on them.

23) Try to establish sources of supply close to home if possible.

24) Don't continue to deal with suppliers who prove to be slow or erratic in making deliveries.

25) Pay all suppliers promptly on receipt of invoices, in order to get the cash discount.

26) Order goods in sufficient quantities to get the best discounts commensurate with your capital.

27) Price your products in such a way that your customers will say they got their money's worth.

28) When selling direct from space ads, offer products in the $10 to $29 price range, and show your prices in round numbers if under $10 and in odd numbers ($19.95) when over $10.

29) Always offer a money-back guarantee on everything you sell.

30) When setting your selling price, figure in all costs relating to the product, not just the cost of the product itself This will include freight in, packing, postage out, etc.

31) Handle only those products that offer a substantial profit margin: not less than forty percent, preferably 100 percent or more.

32) Don't attempt to build a large volume of business with $4 or $7 items. Offer items in the $10 to $50 range, and after you have acquired a customer backlog, start mailing offers of much bigger units of sale.

Make Your Own

ILLUSTRATIONS

33) Don't expect to make a killing, or even a moderate profit, from one ad. Plan to advertise consistently.

34) When using space ads, use a size of ad commensurate with the unit of sale; i.e., a low-priced item usually requires much smaller amounts of space than a relatively high-priced item.

35) It is better to test in two or three magazines than just one, in most situations.

36) Tailor the copy, illustration, and headline of your ad to suit the audience of the magazine you are using.

37) Measure a magazine's effectiveness by what it pulls during a one-month period, and use that figure for determining your cost-per-sale. (Even though, as usually happens, there will be a certain amount of "trickle in" for several months to come.)

38) Determine the number of orders you need to break even, and then use only the magazines which pull above the break-even point.

39) Find your break-even point by dividing your profit margin per unit (determined by subtracting your total unit cost from your selling price) into the cost of the space used.

40) Don't rush to change an ad that is pulling well; experiment regularly, but experiment slowly.

41) Test one thing at a time: first a different headline, then a different illustration, a different price, then a different layout, and so on. If you test more than one thing at a time, you won't know which change produced the different result.

42) Test more than one mailing list at a time if capital permits, but be sure each list is keyed.

43) Offer premiums whenever and wherever you can.

44) Always strive to get a repeat order from a customer who has bought from you at least once. The big profit in mail order is in repeat business.

45) Run an ad that proves to be successful without change until its pull has dropped to the break-even point.

46) If product and ad look good but ad fails to pull, test again with different price, then again with different head. If it still doesn't pull, switch to another product.

47) Don't waste space in a mail order ad; it's too valuable.

48) Small space ads should be written in brief, punchy style with emphasis on facts rather than persuasion.

49) Don't use words or phrases that a mass audience won't understand.

50) Talk about your prospect, not yourself or your company.

51) Strive for conviction and sincerity in ad copy.

52) Give the customer explicit directions for ordering.

53) If you have sufficient profit margin to sell to retail dealers, also ask for dealer inquiries in your space ads; then follow them up with a special dealer mailing.

54) Remember, every letter and package that goes out from you will be the vehicle for circulars and announcements on other products; use them.

55) Get a testimonial program going as soon as you develop a few customers; use best testimonials in ads and letters.

56) Never fail to key an ad, coupon, or order form.

57) If in doubt, get expert help in composing ads and letters.

58) Use illustrations or photographs that show the product in its best light; use them to convey the product's usage, not as ornament.

59) Study the ads in the magazine you are considering, and see how you can design yours to stand out among them.

60) The best mail order magazines and newspapers to use are those that already carry a lot of mail order advertising.

61) In line with the above, the best publications are those that already contain advertisements similar to yours.

62) Newspapers are good for making fast spot tests, but for the long haul your best bet is magazines.

63) As soon as you get a space ad campaign going, have a follow-up customer mailing ready, offering your customers one or more related products. Follow up by direct mail.

64) Right from the beginning set up the names of your customers and inquirers on computers; if you cannot afford this at first, do it as soon as you can.

65) Don't hesitate to rent your customer and inquirer lists to other mail order companies. This is a GREAT source of extra income.

66) Your computer house can file the names of your customers and inquirers alphabetically, geographically, and by year. Make sure each address includes the Zip Code number.

67) Open your own in-house advertising agency as soon as possible.

Advertising

68) Work with an experienced advertising agency in the beginning; ask them show you samples of successful ads and mailings they have produced.

69) Don't expect an advertising agency to work for nothing; they are entitled to ask for flat fees until your ad account grows to the point at which it becomes worthwhile on a fifteen percent commission basis.

70) When an agency-produced ad or campaign goes sour, ask for their opinion and recommendations, then give them a second chance. They may have made fewer mistakes than you think.

71) Don't say, "No C.O.D.'s accepted" in your ads; don't bring it up.

72) Don't be afraid of personal checks; very few of them are returned unpaid. Most people are honest.

73) Don't offer to sell on credit unless you are handling relatively large orders ($300 or more), have sufficient capital to carry the accounts, and have a sufficient profit margin to absorb a five-to-ten percent credit loss.

74) Don't argue with a customer; if she's displeased for any reason, either replace the merchandise or return her money in full.

75) Don't sit on a complaint, thinking it will disappear. (It will just get hotter.) Answer by return mail.

76) If a customer sends you too much money, refund the overpayment immediately. You will make a friend.

77) Work your customer systematically, don't let her cool off. Have something going out regularly—at least once a month if possible.

78) Offer free gifts or premiums to customers who buy more than one product at a time.

79) If an ad or offer is successful for a while and then seems to "wear out," drop it but keep it in the file. After a year or so, it is probable that you can rerun it with the same degree of success it had initially.

80) Keep accurate records of incoming orders and inquiries as to key, date received, etc. This will be invaluable in projecting future ads and campaigns.

81) Maintain accurate business records and accounts so that at any given time you can determine whether you are gaining or losing.

82) Pay special attention to the seasonal aspects of your various offers, expanding your efforts during the peak seasons and cutting back during the off seasons.

Advertising Sales Promotion Agencies

ALABAMA
Dees Communicators Inc.
Fuller Fund Raising Co. 200 S. Huss St.
Montgomery, AL 35104
(205) 263-4436

ARIZONA
Aaron Sauter Gains & Assoc.
Suite D 6511 N. 16th St.
Phoenix, AZ 85016
(602) 265-1933

CALIFORNIA
Thomas/Mail Marketing
P.O. Box 1539
Garden Grove, CA 92642
(714 750-3000

Day Communications
8826 Dorrington Ave.
Los Angeles, CA 90048
(213) 858-0520

Enterprise Agency
3600 South Hill St.
Los Angeles, CA 90007

Muchnick Co.
5818 Venice Blvd.
Los Angeles, CA 90019
(213) 934-7986

The Ad Factory
1888 Century Park, Ste. 216
Los Angeles, CA 90067

Transamerica Financial Corp.
P.O. Box 2494
Los Angeles, CA 90051
(213) 742-4830

Foote Cone & Belding Honig
P.O. Box 3183
San Francisco, CA 94119
(415) 398-5200

Franklin Advertising Inc.
1424 Lincoln Blvd.
Santa Monica, CA 90401
(213) 451-8973

COLORADO
Tracy-Locke Advertising
7503 Marin Dr. #2b
Englewood, CO 80111
(303) 773-3100

CONNECTICUT
Shailer Davidoff Rogers Inc
Heritage Square
Fairfield, CT 06430
(203) 255-3425

Visual Horizons Ltd.
38 Locust Rd.
Greenwich, CT 06830
(203) 531-5208

DISTRICT OF COLUMBIA
Environmental Educators Inc
Ste. 307, 2100 M. St., N.W
Washington, DC 20037
(202) 466-3055

FLORIDA
AANI
11136 Sw. 133 Pl.
Miami, FL 33186
(305) 387-0431

Direct Response Services
5444 Bay Center Dr., Ste. 11
Tampa, FL 33609
(813) 870-1806

GEORGIA
Cable Coupon Network Inc.
2045 Peachtree Rd., Ste. 300
Atlanta, GA 30309
(404) 355-1717

Grizzard Advertising Inc.
1144 Mailing Ave., SW
Atlanta, GA 30315
(404) 622-1501

ILLINOIS
Bernstein & Assoc.
875 N. Michigan, Ste. 1419
Chicago, IL 60611
(312) 440-3700

CPM Inc.
919 N. Michigan Ave.
Chicago, IL 60611
(312) 440-5200

Fisher & Zivi
180 N. Michigan Ave., Rm. 700
Chicago, IL 60601
(312) 236-6226

Flair Communications Agency
214 W. Erie St.
Chicago, IL 60610
(312) 943-5959

HNK & P Direct
333 N. Michigan Ave.
Chicago, IL 60601
(312) 977-9600

Kobs & Brady Advertising Inc.
625 N. Michigan Ave.
Chicago, IL 60611
(312) 944-3500

Lefebvre & Hughes
5545 N. Clark St.
Chicago, IL 60660
(312) 271-4910

Libov Associates
444 N. Michigan Ave.
Chicago, IL 60611
(312) 644-4920

Mandabach & Simms
20 N. Wacker
Chicago, IL 60606
(312) 236-5333

Marcoa Direct Advertising Inc.
10 S. Riverside Plaza
Chicago, IL 60606
(312) 454-0660

INDIANA
Carlson & Co.
3750 Guion Rd.
Indianapolis, IN 46222
(317) 925-7581

IOWA
Broeg and Associates Inc.
1709 W. Washington, Ste. 100
Mt. Pleasant, IA 52641
(319) 986-5144

KANSAS
Brooker Sales Intl. Inc.
P.O. Box 1465
Wichita, KS 67201
(316) 262-7528

LOUISIANA
Benjamin Assoc. Inc.
2736 Florida, P.O. Box 2151
Baton Rouge, LA 70821
(504) 387-0611

MARYLAND
Keary Advertising Co. Inc.
7215 Rolling Mill Rd.
Baltimore, MD 21224
(301) 285-3700

Ketchum MacLeod & Grove
Direct Marketing
11300 Rockville Pike
Rockville, MD 20852

MASSACHUSETTS
Continental Cablevision
Pilot House-Lewis Wharf
Boston, MA 02110
(617) 742-6140

DR Group Inc.
10 Post Office Square
Boston, MA 02109
(617) 482-7300

Reply-O
148 State St., Ste. 508
Boston, MA 02109
(617) 720-1150

Dickinson Direct Response Inc.
67 Federal Ave.
Quincy, MA 02169
(617) 471-9222

MICHIGAN
Ross Roy Inc.
2751 E. Jefferson Ave.
Detroit, MI 48207
(313) 568-6000

MINNESOTA
Larranaga and Associates
7900 Xerxes Ave., South
Bloomington, MN 55431
(612) 835-4520

Advertising Photography
5832 Wooddale Ave., South
Minneapolis, MN

Carlson Mkt. & Movtivation
12755 State Highway 55
Minneapolis, MN 55441
(612) 540-5566

MISSISSIPPI
Direct Mail Specialist Inc.
2012 Highway 90 West
Gautier, MS 39552
(601) 497-4100

MISSOURI
Maritz Inc.
1355 N. Highway Dr.
Fenton, MO 63026
(314) 938-4000

Batz-Hodgson-Neuwoehner Adv.
406 W. 34 St.
Kansas City, MO 64111
(816) 561-7586

Fletcher/Mayo/Associates Inc.
Box B Sta. E. John Glen Rd.
St. Joseph, MO 64505
(816) 233-8261

Advertising Associates Inc.
7750 Clayton Rd.
St. Louis, MO 63117
(314) 644-3880

NEBRASKA
Ayres and Associates Inc.
6800 Normal Blvd.
Lincoln, NE 68506

Interstate Tele-Marketing
P.O. Box 34057
Omaha, NE 68134
(402) 493-2300

NEW JERSEY
Associated Insurance Marketer
Two Executive Campus
Rt. 70 & Cutbert Blvd.
Cherry Hill, NJ 08002
(609) 662-3015

George Bryant and Staff
71 Grand Ave.
Englewood, NJ 07631

Loch Arbour Direct
560 Main St.
Loch Arbour, NJ 07711
(201) 531-0212

Margrace Corporation
300 Chestnut St.
Middlesex, NJ 08846
(201) 469-7550

NEW YORK
Success Advertising Agency
1426 54th St.
Brooklyn, NY 11219
(212) 851-6965

Input Prep Inc.
51 Toledo St.
Farmingdale, NY 11735
(516) 487-9440

Blair Company
185 Great Neck Rd.
Great Neck, NY 11021
(516) 487-9200

Hyaid Inc.
6 Commercial St.
Hicksville, NY 11801
(516) 433-3800

LK Advertising Agency
Putter Bldg.
Middle Island, NY 11953
(516) 924-3888

Adler & Lane
450 Seventh Ave.
New York, NY 10001
(212) 947-8867

Ahrend Associates Inc.
79 Madison Ave.
New York, NY 10016
(212) 685-0033

Albert Frank/FCB
61 Broadway
New York, NY 10006
(212) 248-5200

Allied Graphic Arts Inc.
1515 Broadway
New York, NY 10006
(212) 730-1414

Ayer Direct
1345 Ave. of Americas
New York, NY 10105
(212) 708-6336

Bloom & Gelb Inc.
310 Madison Ave.
New York, NY 10017
(212) 286-1070

Bozell & Jacobs Inc.
#Dag Hammarskjold Plaza
New York, NY 10017
(212) 644-7200

Chapman & Quinn
8th Floor 1270 Broadway
New York, NY 10001
(212) 564-9870

Chapman Direct Marketing Inc.
415 Madison Ave.
New York, NY 10017
(212) 758-8230

Compton Direct Marketing
635 Madison Ave.
New York, NY 10022
(212) 358-7800

D M Group Inc.
477 Madison Ave.
New York, NY 10022
(212) 355-2530

D R Group Inc.
342 Madison Ave.
New York, NY 10017
(212) 687-2100

Franklin & Joseph Inc.
237 Mamaroneck Ave.
White Plains, NY 10605
(914) 997-0212

NORTH CAROLINA
Excalibur Enterprises Inc.
P.O. Box 7372
Winston-Salem, NC 27109
(919) 723-2463

NORTH DAKOTA
Ness Agency Inc.
325 7th St., South
Fargo, ND 58102
(701) 280-1768

OHIO
Robert Silverman Inc.
1375 Euclid Ave.
Cleveland, OH 44115
(216) 771-6322

Simpson Mkt. Comm. Agency
1301 Dublin Rd.
Columbus, OH 43215
(614) 481-8371

Berry and Company
3170 Kettering Blvd.
Dayton, OH 45439
(513) 296-2074

OKLAHOMA
GKD Direct Marketing
1330 Classen Blvd.
Oklahoma City, OK 73146
(405) 232-2333

PENNSYLVANIA
National Mail/Marketing Corp.
97 Cedar Grove Rd.
Media, PA 19063
(215) 353-6733

Ernest Advertising Inc.
3305 Goshen Rd.
Newtown Square, PA 19073
(215) 356-3606

Direct Main Council Inc.
2030 Upland Way
Philadelphia, PA 19131
(215) 477-9700

Hawthorne Advertising Inc.
5 Penn Center Plaza
Philadelphia, PA 19103

Compass Marketing Serv. Inc.
Midtown Towers Penthouse
643 Liberty Ave.
Pittsburgh, PA 15222
(412) 261-1733

Invention Marketing Inc.
701 Smithfield St.
Pittsburgh, PA 15222
(412) 288-1311

RHODE ISLAND
Dial Media Inc.
59 West Shore Rd.
Warwick, RI 02889
(401) 738-5100

TENNESSEE
Gish Sherwood & Friends Inc.
2 International Plaza, Ste. 511
Nashville, TN 37217
(615) 361-7171

TEXAS
Bloom Advertising Agency Inc.
P.O. Box 225975
Dallas, TX 75265
(214) 638-8100

Jolly Co. Inc.
3003 Carlisle, Ste. 112
Dallas, TX 75204
(214) 651-7681

Baxter & Korge Inc.
8323 Westglen
Houston, TX 77063
(713) 781-5110

Executive Marketing Serv. Inc.
360 Garden Oaks Blvd.
Houston, TX 77018
(800) 231-0427

The Photographers Inc.
2121 Regency Dr.
Irving, TX 75062
(214) 438-4114

VERMONT
Direct Communications Corp.
75 Main St.
Fair Haven, VT 05743
(802) 265-8144

VIRGINIA
White Company Inc.
5750b Gen. Washington Dr.
Alexandria, VA 22312
(703) 750-3680

ideas = money

Consultants

CALIFORNIA
Lenca Inc.
9595 Wilshire Blvd.
Beverly Hills, CA 90212
(213) 273-6098

Market-Direct Advertising
P.O. Box 92630-0817
El Toro, CA 92630
(714) 768-5830

Hedberg & Assoc. Inc.
3606 Terrace View Dr.
Encino, CA 91436
(213) 789-2079

Christian Resource Management
3423 E. Chapman, Ste. A
Orange, CA 92669
(714) 997-3920

COLORADO
Maxwell Sroge
731 N. Cascade
Colorado Springs, CO 80903
(303) 633-5556

CONNECTICUT
Cash Flow Inc.
Soundview Farms Exec. Pk.
15 Signal Rd.
Stamford, CT 06902
(203) 356-1387

KDW Direct Marketing Assoc.
14 Windy Hill Rd.
Westport, CT 06880
(203) 226-3892

DISTRICT OF COLUMBIA
The Kamber Group
1899 L St., N.W., Ste. 800
Washington, DC 20036
(202) 223-8700

FLORIDA
Communicomp
P.O. Box 15725
Plantation Post Office
Ft. Lauderdale, FL 33318

American Fraternal Programmer
1100 NE 125th St.
N. Miami, FL 33161
(305) 891-9800

Svenson Company Inc.
3767 Priarie Dunes Dr.
Sarasota, FL 33583
(813) 921-3359

ILLINOIS
Achziger Inc.
Worldbook Childcraft Complex
Merchandise Mart Plaza
Chicago, IL 60654
(312) 245-3068

Association Consultants Inc.
180 N. Lasalle St., Ste. 3220
Chicago, IL 60601
(312) 726-3079

Becker Trading Company
401 N. Michigan AVe.
Chicago, IL 60611
(312) 329-0705

Fenvessy & Kestnbaum
221 N. Lasalle St.
Chicago, IL 60601

INDIANA
Wales & Co.
211 W. Madison St.
P.O. Box 4123
South Bend, IN 46634
(219) 232-4200

IOWA
Broeg and Associates Inc.
1709 W. Washington, Ste. 100
Mt. Pleasant, IA 52641
(319) 986-5144

KANSAS
Ross & Co.
4708 W. 81st St.
Shawnee Mission, KS 66208
(816) 471-5200

Boothe Advertising Agency
1010 N. Main
Wichita, KS 67203
(316) 267-9251

MARYLAND
Absher Direct Marketing
1110 Fidler Ln., Ste. 1410
Silver Spring, MD 20910
(301) 565-0350

MASSACHUSETTS
Response Imperatives Ltd.
79 Federal St.
Newburyport, MA 01950
(617) 462-8324

MINNESOTA
Sonlite Inc.
15500 Wayzata Blvd.
Wayzata, MN 55391
(612) 473-3275

MISSOURI
Midland Mailing Corp.
666 Mason Ridge Center Dr.
St. Louis, MO 63141
(314) 434-0327

NEW HAMPSHIRE
Paul Sampson
Box 100
Freedom, NH 03836
(603) 539-4080

NEW JERSEY
Dick Franklin
76 High St.
Bloomfield, NJ 07003
(201) 338-0295

National Telemarketing Inc.
#2 E. Blackwell St., Ste. 15
Dover, NJ 07801
(201) 361-3500

NEW YORK
Gordon Grossman Inc.
606 Douglas Rd.
Chappaqua, NY 10514
(914) 238-9387

Market Response International
Colonial Bldg.
Clinton, NY 13312
(315) 853-5788

Shepard Associates Inc.
2 Micole Ct.
Dix Hills, NY 11746
(516) 271-5567

Direct Marketing Sys. & Serv.
338 E. Columbus Ave.
E. White Plain, NY 10604
(914) 997-2937

Fairbanks Associates Inc.
199 Jericho Turnpike, Ste. 300
Floral Park, NY 11001
(212) 343-3308

Lieb Direct Marketing
77 Duck Pond Rd.
Glen Cove, NY
(516) 759-2754

The Cowen Group Inc.
205 E. Main St.
Huntington, NY 11743
(516) 673-0099

Richard Silverman
83-33 Austin St.
Kew Gardens, NY 11415
(212) 441-5358

Barclay Studios
5 West 19 St.
New York, NY 10011
(212) 255-3440

Ted Bartek
343 E. 93 St.
New York, NY 10028
(212) 534-4550

Blumenfeld Dir. Mkt. & Adv.
500 Fifth Ave
New York, NY 10036
(354-6818

Crandall Associates
501 Fifth Ave
New York, NY 10017
(212) 687-2550

Direction M Inc.
1385 York Ave.
New York, NY 10021
(212) 988-5110

Kumbles Mkt. Staff
141 E. 44th St.
New York, NY 10017
(212) 661-0320

Betty Anne Noakes
251 E. 51st St., #14j
New York, NY 10022
(212) 688-6840

OHIO
Hamilton Design & Associates
681 Front St.
Columbus, OH 43206
(614) 444-9817

PENNSYLVANIA
Paul Mitson
832 Hamilton Mall, Ste. 1b
Allentown, PA 18101
(215) 776-5015

Albert Direct Marketing
444 Lakeview Ct.
Langhorne, PA 19047
(215) 752-3433

RHODE ISLAND
Weingeroff Enterprises Inc.
One Weineroff Blvd.
Cranston, RI 02910
(401) 467-2200

TEXAS
Select Marketing Company
P.O. Box 4055
Austin, TX 78765
(512) 255-4171

Tucker & Associates
3525 Cedar Springs
Dallas, TX 75219
(214) 528-9210

CFI-DCI
7331 Harwin, Ste. 201
Houston, TX 77036
(713) 784-9391

WASHINGTON
Robert A. Baker
Direct Mail Marketing
Seattle, WA 98177
(206) 542-8431

WISCONSIN
Response Marketing
741 N. Milwaukee St.
Milwaukee, WI 53202
(414) 278-0827

Computer Services

ARKANSAS
CCX
301 Industrial Blvd.
Conway, AR 72032
(501) 329-6836

CALIFORNIA
Creative Mailings Inc.
20850 Leapwood, Stes. C&E
Carson, CA 90746
(213) 532-8296

MS Data Service Corp.
10221 Slater Ave., #112
Fountain Valley, CA 92708
(714) 962-8863

Mailing Data Services Inc.
510 E. Commercial St.
Los Angeles, CA 90012
(213) 626-6301

COLORADO
Neodata Services
1255 Portland Place
Boulder, CO 80302
(303) 442-4282

CONNECTICUT
Blumenfield Marketing Inc.
300 Broad St.
Stamford, CT 06901
(203) 359-2080

DISTRICT OF COLUMBIA
Aztecch Corporation
1621 Connecticut Ave., N.W.
Washington, DC 20009
(202) 232-5500

FLORIDA
Direct Response Services Inc.
5444 Bay Center Dr., Ste. 111
Tampa, FL 33309
(813) 870-1806

GEORGIA
National Data Corp.
One National Plaza
Corporate Square
Atlanta, GA 30329

ILLINOIS
List Processing Company
329 Interstate Rd.
Addison, IL 60101
(312) 543-0100

Computer Marketing Services
333 N. Michigan Ave.
Chicago, IL 60601
(312) 782-7376

Dependable Lists Inc.
333 N. Michigan Ave.
Chicago, IL 60601
(312) 263-3566

MMS Inc.
541 N. Fairbanks Ct.
Chicago, IL 60611
(312) 467-9500

Hallmark Data Systems Inc.
5500 Touhy Ave.
Skokie, IL 60077
(312) 674-6900

KANSAS
Words & Data Inc.
P.O. Box 7529
Overland Park, KS 66207
(913) 649-1276

MARYLAND
Regnis Lam Inc.
P.O. Box 939
Adelphi, MD 20783
(301) 445-3305

Lewis Systems Inc.
335 E. Oliver St.
Baltimore, MD 21202
(301) 962-5454

Systems 80
4733 Bethesda Ave., Ste. 520
Bethesda, MD 20014
(301) 654-5377

Kiplinger Computer & Mailing
3401 East-West Highway
Editors Park, MD 20782
(202) 298-6400

Postal Data Corporation
4007 Hwy. 301
La Plata, MD 20646
(301) 870-3600

Directech Inc.
11300 Rockville Pike
Rockville, MD 20852
(301) 881-0664

ASCC
5104 Frolich Ln.
Tuxedo, MD 20718
(301) 773-3500

MASSACHUSETTS
Epsilon Data Management Inc.
24 New England Exec. Park
Burlington, MA 01803
(617) 273-0250

Upban Data Processing Inc.
209 Middlesex Turnpike
Burlington, MA 01803
(617) 273-0900

MINNESOTA
Computer Services Division
3499 N. Lexington Ave.
St. Paul, MN 55164
(800) 328-9595

MISSOURI
Computer Marketing Services
41 Kimbler Dr.
Hazelwood, MO 63043
(314) 878-4212

NEW JERSEY
Credit Index
170 Mt. Airy Rd.
Basking Ridge, NJ 07920
(201) 766-5000

Data Scribe Inc.
2201 Route 38
Cherry Hill, NJ 08002
(609) 667-6066

Ehrhart-Babic Data Services
120 Rt. 9, West
Englewood Cliffs, NJ 07632
(201) 947-4747

Publishers Computer Corp.
P.O. Box 1100
Fort Lee, NJ 07024
(201) 947-4144

Ready Data Services Inc.
185 Cross St.
Fort Lee, NJ 07024
(201) 461-0382

NEW YORK
Interstate Computer Svcs. Inc.
754 Fourth Ave.
Brooklyn, NY 11232
(212) 965-2500

Type-A-Scan Inc.
1358 Rockaway Pkwy.
Brooklyn, NY 11236
(212) 257-3605

MAGI
3 Westchester Plaza
Elmsford, NY 10523
(212) 697-2720

Fulfillment Associates Inc.
155 Allen Blvd.
Farmingdale, NY 11737
(516) 266-1585

Anchor Computer
750 Zeckendorf Blvd.
Garden City, NY 11530
(212) 695-3600

AM Express Direct Rsps. Div.
175 Community Dr.
Great Neck, NY 11205
(516) 487-0140

H Y Aids Inc.
6 Commercial St.
Hicksville, NY 11801
(516) 433-3800

MBS/Multimode
7 Norden Ln.
Huntington Sta., NY 11746
(516) 673-5600

Target Mailing Services
857 N. Queens Ave.
Lindenhurst, NY 11757
(516) 884-6100

Venezian Inc.
10-64 Jackson Ave.
Long Island, NY 11101
(212) 784-0500

C&L Data Systems
Computers & Labels Inc.
59 Kensico Dr.
Mt. Kisco, NY 10549
(914) 241-2436

AFC Computed Services
370 Seventh Ave.
New York, NY 10001
(212) 564-6400

Enertex Computer Concepts
444 Park Ave., S.
New York, NY 10016
(212) 685-3535

Wiland & Associates Inc.
60 E. 42 St.
New York, NY 10165
(212) 986-8798

OHIO
Data Response Services
P.O. Box 8294
Canton, OH 44711
(216) 494-0285

American Adv. Service
1329 Arlington St.
Cincinnati, OH 45225
(513) 542-7700

Filfillment Corp. of America
205 W. Center St.
Marion, OH 43302
(614) 383-5231

OKLAHOMA
Computer Management Corp.
4515 N. St. Fe
Oklahoma City, OK 73118
(405) 528-2550

PENNSYLVANIA
Data Service Associates
49 Valley
Furlong, PA 18925
(215) 343-6166

Modern Marketing Inc.
99 Buck Rd.
Huntingdon Valley, PA 19006
(215) 355-5270

American Service Assoc.
1965 New Hope St.
Norristown, PA 19401
(212) 275-3724

Electronic Data Proc. Corp.
1520 Locust St.
Philadelphia, PA 19106
(215) 732-9150

SOUTH CAROLINA
Dept. Services Ltd.
P.O. Box 2829
Myrtle Beach, SC 29577
(803) 448-7914

TENNESSEE
NLT Computer Services Corp.
National Life Center
Nashville, TN 37250
(615) 256-7600

TEXAS
Adoniram
P.O. Box 786
Fort Worth, TX 76101
(817) 589-7657

Management Control Systems
P.O. Box 7252
Ft. Worth, TX 76111
(817) 625-4221

UTAH
The Word Shop
136 E. South Temple #2140
Salt Lake City, UT 84111
(801) 521-9563

VIRGINIA
Letters Unlimited
1900 N. Beauregard St.
Alexandria, VA 22311
(703) 998-0338

C.A.C.I.
1815 N. Fort Myer Drive
Arlington, VA 22209

Mail Technology Services
138 Church St.
Vienna, VA 22180
(703) 281-5560

WASHINGTON
Manus Services Corp.
1700 Westlake Ave., N. Ste. 10
Seattle, WA 98109
(206) 285-3260

WISCONSIN
Figis Data Center Inc.
630 S. Central Ave.
Marshfield, Wi 54449
(715) 387-1771

Envelope Manufacturers and Distributors

ARIZONA
Southwest Envelope Co.
3839 N. 35th Ave.
Phoenix, AZ 85017
(603) 272-2691

U.S. Envelope
3316 E. Washington St.
Phoenix, AZ 85034

CALIFORNIA
Gilmore Envelope Corp.
4540 Worth St.
Los Angeles, CA 90063
(213) 268-3401

Golden State Envelopes
1601 Gower St.
Los Angeles, CA 90028
(213) 461-3044

U.S. Envelope
P.O. Box 23928
Los Angeles, CA 90023

Mail-Well Envelope Co.
809 W. Santa Anita St.
San Gabriel, CA 91778
(213) 289-3623

Federal Envelope Co.
660 Forbes Blvd.
So. San Francisco, CA 94080

Federal Envelope Co.
352 Shaw Rd.
So. San Francisco, CA 94080

COLORADO
Federal Envelope Co.
5000 Kingston St.
Denver, CO 80239

Rockmont Envelope Co.
3500 Rockmont Dr.
Denver, CO 80217
(303) 455-3505

CONNECTICUT
U.S. Envelope
180 Moody Rd.
Enfield, CT 06082

GEORGIA
AECO Products Division
P.O. Box 1267
Atlanta, GA 30301
(404) 351-5016

Atlantic Envelope Company
P.O. Box 1267
Atlanta, GA 30301
(404) 351-5011

HAWAII
Mail-Well Envelope Co.
150 Puuhale Rd.
Honolulu, HI 96819
(808) 847-3786

ILLINOIS
Boise Cascade Envelope Div.
313 Rohlwing Rd.
Addison, IL 60101
(312) 620-2828

Continental Envelope Corp.
1301 W. 35th St.
Chicago, IL 60609
(312) 254-3900

Garden City Envelope Company
3001 N. Rockwell St.
Chicago, IL 60618
(312) 267-3600

HECO Envelope
5445 N. Elston Ave.
Chicago, IL 60630
(312) 286-6400

Outlook Envelope Co.
3524 W. Belmont Ave.
Chicago, IL 60618
(312) 583-5838

Transco Envelope Company
3542 N. Kimball Ave.
Chicago, IL 60618
(312) 267-9200

INDIANA
U.S. Envelope
P.O. Box 1346
Indianapolis, IN 46206

IOWA
Tension Envelope Corp.
P.O. Box 1341
Des Moines, IA 50305

U.S. Envelope
700 East 4th St.
Des Moines, IA 50316

MARYLAND
Oles Envelope Corporation
532 East 25th St.
Baltimore, MD 21218
(301) 243-1520

U.S. Envelope
66 Amberton Dr.
Elk Ridge, MD 21227
(301) 796-7880

MASSACHUSETTS
Boston Envelope Company Inc.
150 Royall St.
Canton, MA 02021
(617) 828-6100

New England Envelope Manf. Co.
237 Chandler St.
Worcester, MA 01609
(617) 798-3736

Sheppard Envelope Company
1 Envelope Terrace
Worcester, MA 01613
(617) 791-5588

MICHIGAN
Service Envelope Co.
1301 Harper Ave.
Detroit, MI 48211
(313) 872-6000

MINNESOTA
MacKay/Minnesota Envelopes
2100 Elm St., S.E.
Minneapolis, MN 55414
(612) 331-9311

Tension Envelope Corp.
129 N. 2nd St.
Minneapolis, MN 55401

Continental Envelope Corp.
Mpls.-St. Paul Office
5515 Shore Trail Ne.
Prior Lake, MN 55372
(800) 621-8155

MISSOURI
Envelopes Limited
899 E. 1st St.
Kansas City, MO 64106
(816)421-0531

Tension Envelope Corp.
819 E. 19th St.
Kansas City, MO 64108
(816) 471-3800

St. Regis Envelopes
601 Cannonball Lane
Ofallon, MO 63366
(314) 272-2500

Missouri Encom Inc.
10655 Gateway Blvd.
St. Louis, MO 63132
(314) 994-1300

NEBRASKA
Federal Envelope Co.
915 North 43rd Ave.
Omaha, NE 68131

NEW JERSEY
Berlin & Jones Envelope Co.
2 E. Union Ave.
East Rutherford, NJ 07070
(201) 933-5900

Gotham Envelope Corp.
1 Madison St.
East Rutherford, NJ 07073

Housatonic Valley Paper
15 Exchange Pl.
Jersey City, NJ 07303
(212) 349-1730

Transo Envelope Company
100 Moniter St.
Jersey City, NJ 07304

NEW YORK
Karl Inc., Walter
Package Inserts 135 Bedford Rd.
Armonk, NY 10504
(212) 324-8900

North American Envelope Co.
20 Maple Ave.
Armonk, NY 10504
(914) 273-8620

Envelope Convertors Inc.
100 Morgan Ave.
Brooklyn, NY 11237
(212) 386-6000

General Paper Goods Mfg. Co.
253 36th St.
Brooklyn, NY 11232
(212) 788-2500

Business Envelope Mfgrs. Inc.
900 Grand Blvd.
Deer Park, NY 11729
(516) 242-2500

Commercial Envelope
900 Grand Blvd.
Deer Park, NY 11729
(516) 242-2500

Design Destributors Inc.
45 E. Industry Ct.
Deer Park, NY 11729
(516) 242-2000

U.S. Envelope
2 Westchester Plaza
Elmsford, NY 10523

Boise Cascade Envelope Div.
New York Office 747 Third Ave.
New York, NY 10017
(212) 759-3591

Buffalo Envelope Co.
270 Michigan Ave.
New York, NY 10017

Karolton Envelope Division
209 East 56th St.
New York, NY 10022
(212) 752-8484

Rex Envelope Co. Inc.
74 Charlton St.
New York, NY 10014
(212) 675-9200

Tri-State Envelope Corp.
One Penn Plaza
New York, NY 10001
(212) 564-7750

NORTH CAROLINA
U.S. Envelope
349f West Tremont St.
Charlotte, NC 28203

OHIO
Boise Cascade Envelope Div.
4500 Tiedeman Rd.
Cleveland, OH 44144
(216) 252-4100

Ohio Envelope Manufacturing
5161 W. 164th St.
Cleveland, OH 44142
(216) 267-2920

OREGON
Mail-Well Envelope Co.
2515 Se. Mailwell Dr.
Portland, OR 97222
(503) 654-3141

U.S. Envelope
3215 Northwest Yeon Ave.
Portland, OR 97210

PENNSYLVANIA
Boise Cascade Envelope Div.
7301 Penn. Ave.
Pittsburg, PA 15208
(412) 243-8010

U.S. Envelope
511 Parkway View Dr.
Pittsburgh, PA 15205

TENNESSEE
Tension Envelope Corp.
P.O. Box 30114
Memphis, TN 38130

St. Regis Paper Co.
Consumer Products Div.
820 Seventh Ave. N.
Nashville, TN 37219
(615) 244-2330

TEXAS
Federal Envelope Co.
Hillcrest 635 Ste. 114
Dallas, TX 75230

Love Envelopes Incorporated
1130 Quaker St.
Dallas, TX 75207
(214) 638-5900

Gulf Envelope Company
4340 Director Row P.O. Box 164
Houston, TX 77001
(713) 681-6111

UTAH
Rockmont Envelope Co.
360 W. Bugatti St.
Salt Lake City, UT 84115
(801) 487-9681

VIRGINIA
U.S. Envelope
6829 Atmore Rd.
Richmond, VA 23225

Convertagraphics
7702 Plantation Rd.NW
Roanoke, VA 24019
(703) 362-3311

Double Envelope Corp.
P.O. Box 7000
Roanoke, VA 24019
(703) 362-3311

WASHINGTON
Northwest Envelope Co.
401 Andover Park East
Seattle, WA 98188

WISCONSIN
Continental Envelope Corp.
Madison Office 502 San Juan Trail
Madison, WI 53705
(800) 621-8155

Full Service Printers/Lettershops

ALABAMA
A.G. Response
3500 Independent Dr.
Birmingham, AL 35209
(205) 870-5014

ARIZONA
Advanced Mailing Systems
205 S. Mckemy St.
Chandler, AZ 85224
(602) 893-0101

American Automatic Mailings
336 S. Brooks
Mesa, AZ 85202
(602) 834-5014

ARKANSAS
Schuh Advertising Inc., Lloyd
1007 W. Seventh St.
Little Rock, AR 72203
(501) 374-2332

Wordsworth Company
711 W. 7th St.
Little Rock, AR 72201
(501) 371-0000

CALIFORNIA
Creative Mailings Inc.
20850 Leapwoods Stes. C & E
Carson, CA 90746
(312) 532-8296

Creative Web Systems
371 N. Oak St.
Inglewood, CA 90302
(213) 673-8833

National Adv. & Mkt. Eng.
1352 South Flower
Los Angeles, CA 90015
(213) 748-2241

Lewis & Mayne Inc.
Direction Division 645 Harrison St.
San Francisco, CA 94107
(415) 543-7385

Addresses Unlimited
14621 Titus St.
Van Nuys, CA 91402
(213) 873-4114

CONNECTICUT
Word Communications Systems
41a New London Tpke.
Glastonbury, CT 06033
(203) 659-0528

Baxter Brothers Inc.
1030 E. Putnam Ave.
Greenwich, CT 06830
(203) 637-4559

Volk In., Kurth H.
1755 Boston Post Rd.
Milford, CT 06460
(203) 878-6381

Data-Mail Inc.
510 New Park Ave.
W. Hardford, CT 06110
(203) 233-5531

DISTRICT OF COLUMBIA
Hennage Creative Printers
814 H St. N.W.
Washington, DC 20001
(202) 628-8282

Kiplinger Washington Editors
1729 H St. N.W.
Washington, DC 20006
(202) 298-6400

FLORIDA
Direct Market Concepts
250 Park St.
Jacksonville, FL 32204
(904) 355-5541

Ace-Parker Inc.
3850 N.W. 30th Ave.
Miami, FL 33142
(305) 635-1111

Zenith Communications Group
6599 N.W. 65th Ave.
Miami, FL 33166
(305) 592-6404

Robinsons Incorporated
P.O. Box 7725
Orlando, FL 32854
(305) 898-2808

ILLINOIS
Active Graphics Inc.
548 S. Clark St.
Chicago, IL 60605
(312) 922-6145

Compuletter Inc.
5651 N. Western Ave.
Chicago, IL 60659
(312) 275-5400

INDIANA
Carlson & Company
3750 Guion Rd.
Indianapolis, IN 46222
(317) 925-7581

Mail Marketing Materials Inc.
P.O. Box 41223
211 W. Madison St.
South Bend, IN 46634

MARYLAND
Emptor Mailing Serv.
Div. of Psa Inc. 1008 Russell St.
Baltimore, MD 21203
(301) 685-5388

Tidewater Publishing Corp.
Centreville, MD 21617
(301) 758-1500

MASSACHUSETTS
Hub Mail Advertising
35 Morrissey Blvd.
Boston, MA 02125
(617) 482-6245

Mail Communications Inc.
2401 Revere Beach Pkwy.
Everett, MA 02149
(617) 389-5350

MINNESOTA
McGill/Jensen Inc.
655 Fairview Ave. No.
St. Paul, MN 55014
(612) 645-0751

MISSOURI
Marketing Communications
1650 Broadway
Kansas City, MO 64108
(816) 421-6641

Mediaworks Inc.
300 W. 19th Terrace
Kansas City, MO 64108
(816) 471-3011

Direct Mail Corp. of America
1533 Washington Ave.
St. Louis, MO 63103
(314) 436-1122

NEW JERSEY
Coupon Service Corp.
631 Grove St.
Jersey City, NJ 07302
(201) 659-8888

Pronto Addressing & Mailing
241 Erie St.
Jersey City, NJ 07302

Tudor Graphics Inc.
1 Ryan Dr.
Westville, NJ 08093
(609) 456-3973

NEW YORK
Bonded Mailings Inc.
754 4th Ave.
Brooklyn, NY 11232
(212) 965-2500

Valco Reproduction & Mailing
1535 Hart Pl.
Brooklyn, NY 11224
(212) 372-0100

Accurate Boffer Mail/Mkt. Corp.
32-02 Queens Blvd.
Long Island City, NY 11101
(212) 784-6800

Automatic Mail Services Inc.
3002-48th Ave.
Long Island City, NY 11101
(212) 361-3091

Kane Inc., John M.
22-22 Jackson Ave.
Long Island City, NY 11101
(212) 786-2222

Venezian Inc., A.R.
10-64 Jackson Ave.
Long Island City, NY 11101
(212) 784-0500

Accurate Mail/Marketing Corp.
137 Varick St.
New York, NY 10013
(212) 675-1200

Dillon Agnew & Marton
654 Madison Ave.
New York, NY 10021
(212) 832-2233

Globe Mail Agency
125 W. 24th St.
New York, NY 10011
(212) 675-4600

Harrison Services Inc.
521 Fifth Ave.
New York, NY 10175
(212) 986-6400

OHIO
Excelco Advertising
2157 Crossbough
Toledo, OH 43614
(419) 865-8961

Arnold Graphic Industries Inc.
P.O. Box 257
Uniontown, OH 44685
(216) 896-2365

Motivational Communications
P.O. Box 257
Uniontown, OH 44685
(216) 896-2365

PENNSYLVANIA
Scanforms Inc.
181 Rittenhouse Cir.
Bristol, PA 19007
(215) 785-0101

Speed Mail Service
212 S. Cameron St.
Harrisburg, PA 17101
(717) 238-1444

Modern Marketing Inc.
99 Buck Rd.
Huntingdon Valley, PA 19006
(215) 355-5270

Woodington Mail Adv. Services
810 E. Cayuga St.
Philadelpha, PA 19124
(215) 831-1800

TENNESSEE
Baber & Company, Rodney
303 Madison Ave.
Memphis, TN 38103
(901) 525-6731

TEXAS
Hubler-Roseburg Assoc. Inc.
1405-A Turtle Creek Blvd.
Dallas, TX 75207
(214) 742-2491

Webb Marketing Corp.
2402 Arbuckle Ct.
Dallas, TX 75229
(214) 247-7680

National Graphics
2819 Hillcroft
Houston, TX 77057
(713) 781-5200

Premiere Company, The
2120 Mckinney
Houston, TX 77003
(713) 224-6176

Triway Printers & Mailers Inc.
301 N. Frio
San Antonio, TX 78207
(512) 227-9185

VIRGINIA
Communications Corp. of Amer.
1 Direct Mail Marketing Plaza
Boston, VA 22713
(703) 825-1776

Metro Printing & Mailing Inc.
12000 Sterling Blvd.
Sterling, Virginia 22170
(703) 471-9000

Custom Mailers & Consultants
2400 Westwood Ave.
Richmond, VA 23230
(804) 353-4453

WASHINGTON
Dinner & Klein Inc.
600 S. Spokane St. P.O. Box 3814
Seattle, WA 95124
(206) 682-2494

WISCONSIN
WCUL Services Corp.
10205 W. Greenfield Ave.
Milwaukee, WI 53214
(414) 778-2211

Mailing & Printing Services
1180 American Dr.
Neenah, WI 54956
(414) 722-2333

List Brokers

CALIFORNIA
SPS Inc.
21 Tamal Vista Blvd. Ste. 215
Corte Madera, CA 94925
(415) 927-0444

Marshall Marketing, Hank
P.O. Box 2729
Laguna Hills, CA 92653
(714) 581-5856

Advanced Management Sys. Inc.
Penthouse 9255 Sunset Blvd.
Los Angeles, CA 90069
(213) 858-1520

Volpe-DMS, J.C.
2415 W. 6th St.
Los Angeles, CA 90057
(213) 385-6505

Market Compilation & Research
11633 Victory Blvd.
No. Hollywood, CA 91609
(213) 877-5384

Direct Marketing Associates
7750 Convoy Court #A
San Diego, CA 92111
(714) 560-0666

Names in the News Calif. Inc.
530 Bush St.
San Francisco, CA 94108
(415) 989-3350

General Mailing
644 South B. St.
Tustin, CA 92680
(714) 731-1771

Addresses Unlimited
14621 Titus St.
Van Nuys, CA 91402
(213) 873-4114

COLORADO
Lifestyle Selector, The
1624 Market St.
Denver, CO 80202
(303) 534-5231

CONNECTICUT
A Z List Inforporated
270 Mason St.
Greenwich, CT 06830
(203) 661-3004

DISTRICT OF COLUMBIA
Accredited Mailing Lists Inc.
5272 River Rd.
Washington, DC 20016

Atlantic List Company Inc.
1101 30ths St. N.W. Ste. #109
Washington, DC 20007
(202) 965-6644

Dependable Lists Inc.
1825 J Street N.W.
Washington, DC 20006

List America Inc.
1766 Church St. N.W.
Washington, DC 20036
(202) 265-7815

Transportation Mrkt. Databank
1435 G St. N.W. Suite 815
Washington, DC 20005
(202) 783-7325

FLORIDA
Dunhill Internatnl. List Co. Inc.
2430 W. Oakland Park Blvd.
Ft. Lauderdale, FL 33311
(305) 484-8300

Drey Co. Inc., Alan
104 Crandon Blvd.
Miami, FL 33149

Public Service Research
12900 S.W. 89th Court
Miami, FL 33176
(305) 251-7975

Media Dimensions Inc.
3767 Prairie Dunes Dr.
Sarasota, FL 33581
(813) 921-3359

GEORGIA
Caldwell and Company
Suite E 2025 Peachtree Rd. N.E.
Atlanta, GA 30309
(404) 351-7372

Direct Response Products Inc.
3300 N.E. Expressway
Atlanta, GA 30341
(404) 455-1919

ILLINOIS

Business Mailers Inc.
640 N. Lasalle St.
Chicago, IL 60610
(312) 943-6666

Cahners DM
5 South Wabash Avenue
Chicago, IL 60603

Dependable Lists Inc.
333 N. Michigan Ave.
Chicago, IL 60601
(312) 263-3566

First National List Service
5765 N. Lincoln Ave.
Chicago, IL 60659
(312) 275-4422

G-R-I Corporation
65 E. Southwater St.
Chicago, IL 60601
(312) 977-3700

INDIANA
Burr & Company, Ronald E.
P.O. Box 553
Bloomington, IN 47402
(812) 334-0295

MARYLAND
ADW/ADVO Inc.
10700 Hanna St.
Beltsville, MD 20705
(301) 937-4300

Custom List Services Inc.
4710 Auth Pl. Ste. 675
Camp Springs, MD 20023
(301) 899-6775

MASSACHUSETTS
Commercial Mailing Lists
1000 Worchester Rd. P.O. Box 951
Framingham, MA 01701
(617) 879-2647

MICHIGAN
Polk & Co., R.L.
6400 Monroe Blvd.
Taylor, MI 48180
(313) 292-3200

MINNESOTA
Benway Marketing Inc.
474 2nd St.
Excelsior, MN 55331
(612) 474-1138

MISSISSIPPI
Midsouth Stockman-Farmer
P.O. Box 9607
Jackson, MS 39206
(601) 981-4805

MISSOURI
Heart of America List Co. Inc.
929 S. 7 Hwy. White Oaks Plaza
Blue Springs, MO 64015
(815) 229-5620

Market Development Corp.
41 Kimler Dr.
Hazelwood, MO 63043
(314) 878-4212

NEBRASKA
Metromail Corporation
901 W. Bond St.
Lincoln, NE 68521

NEW HAMPSHIRE
Guild Company
Div. of Mail Marketing Inc.
121 Nashua Rd.
Bedford, NH 03102
(603) 472-8456

NEW JERSEY
CAMA
6 Old Cranbury Rd.
Cranbury, NJ 08512
(609) 443-1298

Consumers Adv. & Marketing
Assoc.
6 Old Cranbury Rd.
Cranbury, NJ 08512
(609) 443-1298

Crane Associates Corp., Charles
1 Executive Dr.
Fort Lee, NJ 07024
(201) 944-2240

Guild Company, The
171 Terrace St.
Haworth, NJ 07641
(201) 387-1023

NEW YORK
M/D/A List Brokerage Co.
Hardscrabble Rd.
Croton Falls, NY 10519
(914) 277-5558

Belth Associates Inc.
971 Richmond Rd.
East Meadow, NY 11554
(516) 483-3030

Fulfillment Associates Inc.
155 Allen Blvd.
Farmingdale, NY 11735
(516) 249-0860

Gale Associates Inc., Saul
57-03 Kissena Blvd.
Flushing, NY 11355
(212) 353-5757

Creative Mailing Lists
1100 Stewart Ave.
Garden City, NY 11530
(516) 832-2510

Lillian Vernon, Inc.
510 S. Fulton Avenue
Mt. Vernon, NY 10550

Religious Lists
43 Maple Ave.
New City, NY 10956
(914) 634-8724

Accredited Mailing Lists Inc.
3 Park Ave.
New York, NY 10016
(212) 889-1180

Accu-List
137 Varick St.
New York, NY 10013
(212) 741-8700

Alen Drey Co. Inc.
600 Third Ave.
New York, NY 10016
(212) 697-2160

Burnett Consultants Inc., Ed
2 Park Ave.
New York, NY 10016
(212) 679-0630

CELCO
381 Park Ave. So. Ste. 919
New York, NY 10016
(212) 684-1881

Charter Select Services
641 Lexington Ave.
New York, NY 10022
(212) 872-8000

Collidge Company Inc., The
25 West 43rd St.
New York, NY 10036

Dependable List Compilation
257 Park Ave. S.
New York, NY 10010
(212) 677-6760

Zeller & Letica Inc.
15 E. 26th St.
New York, NY 10010
(212) 685-7512

OHIO
Klein & Assoc. Inc., John
23632 Mercantile Rd.
Cleveland, OH 44122
(216) 831-0450

OKLAHOMA
Direct Media Inc.
3414 S. Broadway
Edmond, OK 73034
(405) 348-8651

PENNSYLVANIA
Oxford Consumer Inc.
1432 County Line Rd.
Huntington Valley, PA 19006
(215) 364-0566

TEXAS
American Direct Marketing Ser.
2636 Walnut Hill Lane 337
Dallas, TX 75229
(214) 358-4626

VIRGINIA
American Mailing Lists Corp.
7777 Leesburg Pike
Falls Church, VA 22043
(703) 893-2340

Omega List Company
8300 Old Courthouse Rd.
Vienna, VA 22180
(703) 821-1890

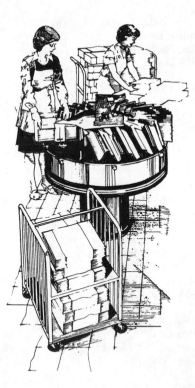

Models and Talent

CALIFORNIA
Abrams-Rubaloff & Assoc. Inc.
9012 Beverly Blvd.
Los Angeles, CA 90022
(213) 273-5711

BCI Casting
9200 Sunset Blvd.
Los Angeles, CA 90069
(213) 550-0156

Blanchard Agency, Nina
1717 N. Highland Ave.
Los Angeles, CA 90028
(213) 462-7274

Celebrity Look-Alikes
9000 W. Sunset Blvd.
Los Angeles, CA 90069
(213) 273-5565

Commercials Unlimited
7461 Beverly Blvd.
Los Angeles, CA 90036
(213) 937-2220

Cronin Bernyce & Assocs.
439 S. La Cienega Blvd.
Los Angeles, CA 90048
(213) 273-8144

Dale Intl. Agent, Garrick
8831 Sunset Blvd.
Los Angeles, CA 99069
(213) 657-2661

DISTRICT OF COLUMBIA
Adair Agency, The
3288 M St. N.W.
Washington, DC 20007
(202) 296-1570

Central Casting
1000 Connecticut Ave. N.W.
Washington, DC 20036
(202) 659-8272

Schwabs Model Store, Anne
3122 N St. N.W.
Washington, DC 20007
(202) 333-3560

NEW YORK
Barbizon Agency of Rego Pk.
95-20 63rd Rd.
New York, NY 10023
(212) 275-2100

BCI Casting
1500 Broadway
New York, NY 10023
(212) 221-1583

Big Beauties Unlimited
336 Central Park W.
New York, NY 10025
(212) 864-0662

Bloom, Michael J.
400 Madison Ave.
New York, NY 10017
(212) 832-6900

Bonie Kid
250 W. 57th St.
New York, NY 10107
(212) 246-0223

Cereghetti Agency
119 W. 57th St.
New York, NY 10019
(212) 765-5260

Charisma Booking Agency
74 Trinity Pl.
New York, NY 10006
(212) 825-0745

Chateau Theatrical Animals
608 W. 48th St.
New York, NY 10036
(212) 246-0520

Chinetti International Motors
1100 Second Ave.
New York, NY 10022
(212) 838-0766

Clair Casting
62 W. 45th St.
New York, NY 10036
(212) 354-7733

Coleman-Rosenberg
667 Madison Ave.
New York, NY 10021
(212) 838-0734

Cooper Assoc, Bill
16 E. 52nd St.
New York, NY 10022
(212) 758-6491

Cunningham & Assoc. Wm. D.
919 Third Ave.
New York, NY 10022
(212) 832-2700

Dawn Animal Agency Inc.
160 W. 46th St.
New York, NY 10036
(212) 575-9396

DMI Talent Assoc.
250 W. 57th St.
New York, NY 10107
(212) 246-4650

Double Take
1501 Broadway
New York, NY 10036
(212) 354-4250

Draper Agency, Stephen
37 W. 57th St.
New York, NY 10019
(212) 421-5780

Elite Model Mgmt. Corp.
150 E. 58th St.
New York, NY 10022
(212) 888-6299

Face to Face
230 Park Ave.
New York, NY 10169
(212) 697-6875

Specialized Media

CALIFORNIA
Marketing Bulletin Board
924 Anacapa St.
Santa Barbara, CA 93101
(805) 963-3111

National Sales Marketing Corp.
924 Anacapa St.
Santa Barbara, CA 93101
(805) 963-8888

FLORIDA
National Enquirer
Lantana, FL 33464
(305) 586-1111

ILLINOIS
Carlyle Marketing Corporation
The Carlyle Building
5850 N. Lincoln Ave.
Chicago, IL 60659
(312) 271-2700

Chicago Sun-Times
401 N. Wabash Ave.
Chicago, IL 60611
(312) 321-2418

Cosmetique Beauty Club
5320 N. Kedzie Ave.
Chicago, IL 60625
(312) 583-5410

Home Shopping Show Inc., The
875 N. Michigan Ave.
Chicago, IL 60611
(312) 951-5111

NEW YORK
Karl Inc., Walter
135 Bedford Rd.
Armonk, NY 10504
(212) 324-8900

Better Homes & Gardens
750 Third Ave.
New York, NY 10017
(212) 557-6531

Blank Associates Inc., Edward
71 West 23 St.
New York, NY 10010
(212) 741-8133

Boys Life & Scouting Magazine
271 Madison Ave.
New York, NY 10016
(212) 532-0985

Cable TV Magazine Inc.
24 W. 40th St.
New York, NY 10018
(212) 687-9788

CBS Publications: Spcl. Marktng.
1515 Broadway
New York, NY 10036
(212) 975-7216

Cosmopolitan Magazine
224 W. 57th St.
New York, NY 10019
(212) 262-6966

Direct Mail Promotors Inc.
342 Madison Ave.
New York, NY 10017
(212) 687-1910

Family Circle Magazine Inc.
488 Madison Ave.
New York, NY 10022
(212) 593-8030

Family Weekly Inc.
641 Lexington Ave.
New York, NY 10022
(212) 980-3000

Geller Assoc., David
535 5th Ave.
New York, NY 10017
(212) 986-8993

House Beautiful Magazine
717 Fifth Ave.
New York, NY 10022
(212) 935-8544

Impact Media Inc.
477 Madison Ave.
New York, NY 10022
(212) 751-7065

John Blair Marketing Inc.
717 Fifth Ave.
New York, NY 10022
(212) 980-5252

List Technology Systems Group
14 Wall St. 9th Floor
New York, NY 10005
(212) 878-9632

Telephone 800 Services

ARIZONA
National Switchboard, The
2150 E. Thomas Rd.
Phoenix, AZ 85016
(602) 955-9710

CALIFORNIA
National Communications Ctr.
3939 Cambridge Rd. Suite 104
Shingle Springs, CA 95682
(916) 677-2254

ILLINOIS
Ring America
6200 N. California Ave.
Chicago, IL 60659
(312) 338-8700

Tele America Inc.
1955 Raymond Dr.
Northbrook, IL 60062
(213) 381-8491

IOWA
Budget Marketing Inc.
1171 7th St.
Des Moines, IA 50314
(515) 243-7000

MARYLAND
Sturner & Klein
11900 Parklawn Dr. Suite 412
Rockville, MD 20852
(301) 881-2720

MINNESOTA
Teletrack Response Center Inc.
Corporate Woods
1111 Douglas Dr. N. Ste. 103
Minneapolis, MN 55422
(612) 541-9100

NEBRASKA
Wats Marketing of America Inc.
3250 N. 9th St.
Omaha, NE 68134
(402) 571-5200

NEVADA
Communication Response Serv.
140 Washington St.
Reno, NV 89503
(800) 648-5309

NEW JERSEY
Mar-Tel Communications Inc.
375 S. Washington Ave.
Bergenfield, NJ 07621
(201) 385-7171

Contact Marketing Inc.
120 Brighton Rd.
Clifton, NJ 07012
(201) 778-7722

National Telemarketing Inc.
2 E. Blackwell St. Suite 15
Dover, NJ 07801
(201) 361-3500

General Telephonics Corp.
7000 Boulevard E.
Guttenberg, NJ 07093
(201) 868-1116

New Resi-Data Marketing Inc.
365 Broadway
Hillsdale, NJ 07642
(201) 666-2212

NEW YORK
Avis Telecommunications
900 Old Country Rd.
Garden City, NY 11530
(516) 222-3800

S & V Communications Group
10-64 Jackson Ave.
Long Island City, NY 11101
(212) 784-0500

C&L Data Sys. Computers & Labl.
59 Kensico Dr.
Mount Kisco, NY 10549
(212) 324-2470

Answer America Inc.
One Park Plaza
New York, NY 10004
(212) 482-6858

Blank Associates Inc., Edward
71 W. 23rd St.
New York, NY 10010
(212) 741-8133

PENNSYLVANIA
American Tele Response Group
511 Abbott Dr.
Broomall, PA 19008
(215) 543-2100

Private Label Companies

Readi-Bake, Inc.
190 28th St. S.E.
Grand Rapids, MI 49510
(616) 241-2631
Products: Frozen Cookie Dough,
Frozen Fruit Filled Turnovers,
Frozen Bread & Roll Doughs, Sweet
Roll Dough, Danish (Cheese, Bow
Ties, Miniature), Buttermilk Biscuits

Realex Corp.
P.O. Box 78
Kansas City, MO 64141
Products: Household Insecticides,
Lawn & Garden Insecticides &
Herbicides

Red Pelican Food Products
5650 St. Jean Detroit, MI 48213
Products: Prepared Mustard,
Distilled Vinegar, Wine Vinegar

The Red Wing Co., Inc.
196 Newton St.
Fredonia, NY 14063
(716) 672-4321
Products: Preserves & Jellies,
Peanut Butter, Catsup & Chili
Sauce, Pancake & Chocolate Syrup,
Spoonable & Pourable Dressings,
Spaghetti & Barbecue Sauce

Reedsburg Foods Corp.
P.O. Box 270
Reedsburg, WI 53959
(608) 524-2346
Products: Canned Peas, Canned
Corn, Canned Green Beans & Wax
Beans

Wm. B. Reily & Co., Inc.
640 Magazine St.
New Orleans, LA 70130
(504) 524-6131
Products: Regular Coffee, Instant

Republic Drug Co., Inc.
175 Great Arrow St.
Buffalo, NY 14207
(716) 874-5060
Products: Generic Drugs, Over-the-
Counter Drugs, Cough Syrups,
Vitamins, Parasiticides

Reynolds Metals Co.
6603 W. Broad St.
Richmond, VA 23261
(804) 281-4678
Products: Aluminum Foil, Aluminum Foil Containers, Plastic Bags,
Heatable

Rich Products Corp.
1150 Niagara St.
Buffalo, NY 14213
(716) 878-8000
Products: Frozen Non-Dairy Coffee
Creamers, Frozen Whipped
Toppings, Frozen Bread Dough

Richheimer Coffee Co.
1127 N. Halsted
Chicago, IL 60622
(312) 787-8352
Products: Coffee, Tea

Ridgeway Hosiery Mills
350 Fifth Ave.
Suite 3719
New York, NY 10118
(212) 594-5466
Products: Ladies Sheer Hosiery

Riegel Textile Corp. Convenience
Products Div.
P.O. Box 929
Aiken, SC 29801
(800) 845-3001
Products: Disposable Diapers,
Moist Towlettes (Baby and All
Purpose), Baby Shampoo, Baby Oil
and Lotion, Baby Powder, Hair-
spray and Hair Conditioning Rinses

Riviana Foods, Inc.
P.O. Box 2636
Houston, TX 77001
(713) 529-3251
Products: Instant Rice

Rockline, Inc.
813 So. Commerce St.
Sheboygan, WI 53081
(414) 452-3004
Products: Coffee Filters

W.B. Roddenbery Co., Inc.
17 First Ave., N.E.
P.O. Box 60
Cairo, GA 31728
(912) 377-2102
Products: Pickles & Relishes,
Peanut Butter, Table Syrups

Roman Cleanser Co.
2700 E. McNichols
Detroit, MI 48077
(313) 891-0700
Products: Bleach, Liquid Laundry
Detergent, Fabric Softener, Dish
Detergent, Ammonia, Window
Cleaner

Rondex Laboratories
200 Elmora Ave.
Elizabeth, NJ 07207
(201) 527-9100
Products: Generic Drugs, First Aid
Products, Ointments & Creams,
Over-the-Counter Drugs, Proprie-
tary Remedies, Vitamins & Food
Supplements

Rose Confections, Inc.
700 Berkshire Lane
Plymouth, MN 55441
(612) 546-8395
Products: Real Semi-Sweet Choco
late Chips, Chocolate Flavored
Baking Chips, Other Flavored
Baking Chips, Sweetened Coconut
(Flakes & Shreds), Packaged Candy

Rose Laboratories
168 Cottage Road
Madison, CT 06443
(203) 245-1210
Products: Suppositories, Ano Rectal
Pharmaceuticals, Contraceptives,
Generic Ointments & Creams, Face
and Body Lotions

Frank T. Ross & Sons, Inc.
P.O. Box 248
West Hill, Ontario
Canada M1E 4R5
(416) 282-1108
Products: All Purpose Cleaners,
Detergetns, Shampoo, Adhesives,
Paint

Roure Bertrand Dupont, Inc.
1775 Windsor Road
Teaneck, NJ 07666
(201) 833-2300
Products: Fragrance for Soaps,
Detergents, Toiletries

Royalace Division (Millen
Industries, Inc.)
93 North Ave.
Garwood, NJ 07027
(800) 526-4280
Products: Paper Doilies, Paper
Placemats, Non-adhesvie Paper
Lining, Adhesive Paper Lining
Paper, Vinyl Lining Paper, Nut
Cups

Russell Corporation
Lee St.
Alexander City, AL 35010
Products: T-Shirts, Sweatshirts,
Sweatpants, Jog-Coordinates,
Shorts

Ryt-Way Packaging Corp.
801 West Fifth St.
P.O. Box 537
Northfield, MN 55057
(507) 645-9503
Products: Instant Milk, Hot Cocoa
Mix, Iced Tea, Dry Drink Mix,
Contract Food Packaging

Sahagian & Associates
115 N. Oak Park Ave.
Oak Park, IL 60301
(312) 848-5552
Products: Lip Balm & Ice, Tooth-
paste & Dentifrice, Hair Care
Products, Skin Creams,
Deodorants, Mouthwash

Salada Foods, Inc.
235 Porter St.
Battle Creek, MI 49016
(616) 966-2320
Products: Tea Bags, Iced Tea Mix,
Instant Tea, Gelatins, Puddings, Pie
Fillings

Sales-Pak, Inc.
2024 Powers Ferry Road
Atlanta, GA 30339
(404) 955-4455
Products: Frozen French Fries,
Whipped Toppings, Seafood,
Frozen Waffles, Frozen Donuts,
Frozen Juices

Salvati Food Produts Co., Inc.
4110 Park Ave.
Bronx, NY 10457
Products: Wine Vinegar, White
Vinegar, Cooking Wines, Spices &
Seasonings

San Antonio Foreign Trading Co.
306 W. Rhapsody
San Antonio, TX 78211
(512) 349-2453
Products: Frozen Cauliflower,
Frozen Broccoli, Frozen Asparagus,
Frozen Okra, Canned Jalapeno
Peppers

San Giorgio-Skinner Co.
One Chocolate Ave.
Heshey, PA 17033
(717) 534-5555
Products: Spaghetti, Thin Spaghetti,
Elbow Macaroni, Noodles, Lasagne,
Capellini

Sandra Tea & Coffee Ltd.
2530 Stanfield Road
Mississauga, Ontario,
Canada L4Y 1S4
Products: Tea, Coffee, Instant
Coffee, Non-Dairy Creamer

John B. Sanfilippo & Son, Inc.
2299 Busse Road
Elk Grove Village, IL 60007
Products: Dry Roasted Nuts, Oil
Roasted Nuts, Peanut Butter,
Snacks

Sanford Chemical Co., Inc.
1945 Touhy Ave.
Elk Grove, IL 60007
(312) 437-3530
Products: Bleach, Cleaners, Deter
gents, Fabric Softeners, Soap

Sather's Inc.
Sather's Plaza
Round Lake, MN 56167
(507) 945-8181
Products: Candy, Cookies, Choco-
late Chips, Coconut, Natural
Foods, Nuts

Sau-Sea Foods, Inc.
1000 Saw Mill River Road
P.O. Box 694
Yonkers, NY 10702
(914) 969-5922
Products: Shrimp Cocktail, Cooked
Shrimp

C.F. Sauer Co.
2000 W. Broad St.
Richmond, VA 23220
Products: Salad Products, Peanut
Butter, Margarine, Vegetable Oils,
Spices, Extracts & Flavorings

Scheer Foods, Inc.
P.O. Box 1688
Savannah, GA 31402
(803) 784-2174
Products: Black Pepper, Salt
Substitutes

Schmit Laboratories, Inc.
1301 W. 35th St.
Chicago, IL 60609
Products: Health and Beauty Aids

The Schrafft Candy Co.
529 Main St.
Boston, MA 02124
(617) 242-2700
Products: Bagged Candy, Box
Chocolates, Thin Mints

Schreiber Foods, Inc.
425 Pine St.
P.O. Box 610
Green Bay, WI 54305
(414) 437-7601
Products: Cheese Products
(Natural, Process, and Imitation)

Schultz & Burch Biscuit Co.
1133 W. 35th St.
Chicago, IL 60609
(312) 927-6622
Products: Toaster Pastries, Crackers

Scothalls Ltd.
997 Decarie Blvd., St. Laurent
Montreal, Quebec,
Canada H4L 3M7
(514) 336-4725
Products: Absorbent Cotton Rolls,
Cotton Gauze, First Aid Products

Seabrook Foods Sales Cooperative
4974 East Clinton Way
Fresno, CA 93747
(209) 252-2836
Products: Frozen Vegetables,
Frozen Fruit

Sealright Co., Inc.
605 W. 47th St.
Kansas City, MO 64112
(816) 531-6666
Products: Containers & Closures,
Packaging

Seamark Corp.
64 Long Wharf
Boston, MA 02110
(617) 364-6700
Products: North Atlantic Seafoods

Sebring Forest Industries
1155 Allied Drive
Sebring, OH 44672
(216) 938-9821
Products: Fireplace Logs, Charcoal
Starter, Kerosene

Senoret Chemical Co.
566 Leffingwell
Kirkwood, MO 63122
(314) 966-2394
Products: Toilet Bow Cleaners,
Cosmetics, Insecticides, Room &
Carpet Deodorizers, Liquid Soap

Sentinel Consumer Products
7750 Tyler Blvd.
Mentor, OH 44060
(216) 974-8144
Products: Cosmetic Puffs, Cosmetic
Squares & Rounds, Cotton Swabs,
First Aid Kits, Footcare Insoles,
Napkins & Sanitary Shields

Sesame Press, Inc.
41 Union Square West
New York, NY 10003
Products: Labels

Sessions Co.
201 West Lee St.
Enterprise, AL 36330
(205) 347-9551
Products: Peanut Butter

Setco, Inc.
3525 Eastham Drive
Culver City, CA 90230
(213) 870-5981
Products: Containers & Closures,
Plastic Bottles

112

Sethness-Greenleaf, Inc.
3645 N. Sacramento Ave.
Chicago, IL 60639
(312) 889-1400
Products: Baking Extracts, Baking
Needs, Extracts, Flavorings, Vanilla

Seymour Canning Co.
P.O. Box 5
Seymour, WI 54165
(414) 833-2371
Products: Canned Peas, Canned
Green Beans, Canned Corn,
Sauerkraut, Canned Beets, Canned
Carrots

Seymour of Sycamore, Inc.
917 Crosby Ave.
Sycamore, IL 60178
(815) 895-9101
Products: Aerosol Spray Paint,
Aerosol Chemicals (Industrial)

Shasta Beverages
2901 Finley Road
Downers Grove, IL 60137
Products: Soft Drinks

Shedd Food Products
2440 S. Floyd St.
Louisville, KY 40217
(502) 637-3631
Products: Peanut Butter, Spanish
Olives, Maraschino Cherries, Prune
Juice

Sheffield Tube Corp.
170 Boad St.
New London, Ct 06320
(203) 442-4451
Products: Toothpaste, Brushless
Shave Cream, Diaper Rash Cream,
Rectal Ointments, Hydrocortisone
Creams & Ointments, Antibiotic
Ointments

Shenandoah Apple Co-Operative,
P.O. Box 435
Winchester, VA 22601
(703) 662-0331
Products: Apple Sauce, Apple
Juice, Sweet Apple Cider, Sliced

Apples, Pure Apple Cider Vinegar,
White Distilled Vinegar, Apples

The Sherwin Williams Co.
Consumer Div.
1370 Ontario St.
Cleveland, OH 44113
(216) 566-3116
Products: Interior/Exterior
Architectural Paints, Varnishes,
Enamels

Shima American Corp.
398 W. Wrightwood Ave.
Elmhurst, IL 60126
(312) 833-9400
Products: Cosmetic Puffs, Foot
Care Insoles, Nail Care Products,
Skin Care Needs

Sid's Sunflower Seed Ltd.
1445 Ottawa St.
Regina, Saskatchewan,
Canada S4R 1N1
(306) 352-8566
Products: Roasted & Salted Sun-
flower Seeds, Roasted & Salted
Sunflower Kenels, Roasted & Salted
Pumpkin Seeds

Silvercreek Foods
P.O. Box 42
Flemington, NJ 08822
(201) 782-4946
Products: Seasoned Stuffing, Dehy
drated Soups, Onion Soup/Dip
Mix, Powdered Drink Mixes,
Blended Seasoning

Silvermills Foods Ltd.
505/10 Iroquois Shore Road
Oakville, Ontario,
Canada L6H 2R3
(416) 845-1017
Products: Baking Powder, Hot
Chocolate, Chicken Coating,
Puddings, Hamburger Dinner
Mixes, Bread Crumbs

Simpak Corporation
2021 15th Ave. West
Seattle, WA 98119
(800) 426-2846
Products: Vitamins, Oral Over-the-
Counter Drugs

Sinole, Inc.
21 Walnut Ave.
Clark, NJ 07066
(201) 499-0102
Products: Vitamins & Dietary
Supplements

Smithfield Farms, Inc.
1801 South Church St.
Smithfield, VA 23430
(804) 357-2145
Products: Barbecue Sauce, Whole
Hog Sausage, Frozen Sandwiches

H.M. Smyth Co., Inc.
P.O. Box 43669
St. Paul, MN 55164
(612) 646-4544
Products: Designers & Consultants,
Labels & Labelers, Printing &
Lithography

So-White Chemical Co., Inc.
5148 Highway 54
Plover, WI 54467
Products: Household Bleach, Fabric
Rinse, Fabric Softener Concentrate,
Ammonia, Vinegars, Swimming
Pool Chlorine

Solinco (Div. of Chock Full
O'Nuts)
425 Lexington Ave.
New York, NY 10017
Products: Instant Coffee, Roast
Coffee

Soluble Products Corp.
480 Oberlin Avenue South
Lakewood, NJ 08701
(201) 364-8855
Products: Instant Breakfast, Cocoa,
Diet Foods, Chocolate Mix Drinks,
Breakfast Drink Mixes

Sona Food Products
3712 Cerritos Ave.
Los Alamitos, CA 90720
Products: Ketchup, Taco Sauce
Soy Sauce, Cooking Oils

Sorento Cheese Co., Inc.
2375 South Park Ave.
Buffalo, NY 14220
(716) 823-6262
Products: Cheese, Dairy Products

The South Seas Trading Co.
P.O. Box 6053
Woodland Hills, CA 91365
(213) 883-4691
Products: Natural Sun Tan Oil
Products

Southern Drying Foods
5202 South Lois Ave.
Tampa, Fl 33611
Products: Breading, Batter Mixes,
Bread Crumbs, Muffin Mixes

Southeast Packaging Corp.
701 Wharton Circle
Atlanta, GA 30336
Products: Household Aerosol Prod-
ucts, Personal Aerosol Products,
Household Liquid Products,
Personal Liquid Products

Southern Food Products Co., Inc.
5353 Downey Road
Vernon, CA 90058
(213) 581-0171
Products: Cookies, Cakes, Snacks,
Granola Bars

Southern Frozen Foods (Div.
Curtice Burns, Inc.)
P.O. Box 306
Montezama, GA 31063
(912) 472-8101
Products: Southern Vegetables,
Breaded Vegetables, Onion Rings

Southern Tea Company
1267 Cobb Industrial Drive
Marietta, GA 30066
(414) 428-5555
Products: Tea Bags, Iced Tea Mix,
Instant Tea, Soft Drink Mixes,
Breakfast Drink Mixes, Chocolate
Drink Mixes

Southland Frozen Foods, Inc.
One Linden Place
Great Neck, NY 11021
(516) 466-3200
Products: Green Beans, Okra,
Southern Greens, Blackeye Peas,
Stew Vegetables, Soup Mix
Vegetables

Sovex Natural Foods, Inc.
9104 Apison Pike
P.O. Box 310
Collegedale, TN 37315
(615) 396-3145
Products: Breakfast Cereals, Snacks

Spada Dist. Co., Inc.
1137 S.E. Union Ave.
Portland, OR 97214
Products: Pasta, Popcorn, Frozen
French Fries, Frozen Vegetables,
Fresh Vegetables

Speaco Corp.
2400 Nicholson Ave.
Kansas City, MO 64120
(816) 474-4884
Products: Vinegar, Apple Juice,
Apple Cider

Specialty Food Packing—Importing
2035 N. 15th Ave.
P.O. Box 1564
Melrose Park, IL 60160
(312) 344-0066
Products: Maraschino Cherries,
Spanish Green Olives, Pepperoncini

Specialty Foods
P.O. Box 5367
Grand Central Station
New York, NY 10017
(800) 223-1920; (212) 986-7220
Products: Beef Stew, Chili with
Beans, Chili without Beans, Corned
Beef Hash, Corned Beef, Luncheon
Meat

Specialty Packaging Products (Div.
of Ethyl Products Co.)
P.O. Box 2448
Richmond, VA 23218
(804) 788-6124
Products: Trigger Sprayers, Finger
Pumps, Soap/Lotion Dispensers,
Tamper Resistant Closures, Metal
Cans, Decorative Metal Caps and
Collars

Stacey Brothers Ltd.
100 St. George St.
Mitchell, Ontario,
Canada N0K 1N0
(519) 348-8414
Products: Butter, Instant Skim
Milk, Margarine

Stahl Soap Corp.
1413 Willow AVe.
Hoboken, NJ 07030
(201) 653-1636
Products: Unwrapped Hard Milled
Soap, Wrapped Hard Milled Soap,
Floating Soap, Pumice Soap,
Laundry Bar Soap

Standard Milling Co.
1009 Central St.
Kansas City, MO 64141
(816) 221-8200
Products: Charcoal Briquettes,
Enriched Cream Farina

Stanley Home Products, Inc. (Nat'l
Contracts Div.)
116 Pleasant St.
Easthampton, MA 01027
(413) 527-1000
Products: Household Chemicals,
Health & Beauty Aids, Hairbrushes,
Mops, Household Brooms

Stanson Detergents
P.O. box 100
Teaneck, NJ 07666
(201) 836-2255
Products: Agglomerated Dishwasher
Detergent, Laundry Detergent, High
Suds Laundry Detergent, Concen
trated Low Suds Laundry Deter
gent, All Frabric Dry Bleach, Bath
Oil Beads

Stephan Co.
1850 W. McNab Road
Ft. Lauderdale, FL 33309
(305) 971-0600
Products: Shampoo, Hair Spray,
Creme Rinse, Hair Conditioner,
Styling Spray, After Shave Lotion

Stephan Chemical Co.
Edens & Winnetra
Northfield, IL 60093
(312) 446-7500
Products: Surfactant Raw Materials
& Concentrates for Cleaners, Deter-
gents, Soaps and Shampoo

Stokely Van-Camp, Inc. (Industrial
Products Group)
525 W. First Ave.
P.O. Box 569
Columbus, OH 43216
(614) 299-3131
Products: Soy, Corn, Sun Salad
Oils, Pure Vegetable Shortening,
Margarine

W.F. Straub Co.
5520 Northwest Highway
Chicago, IL 60630
(312) 763-5520
Products: Honey, Prune Juice,
Molasses

Strout Plastics, Inc.
9611 James Ave. So.
Bloomington, MN 55431
(612) 881-8673; (800) 328-4556
Products: Heatable Plastic Bags &
Wraps, Polyethylene Film
Specialists

A. Sturm & Sons, Inc.
977 Depot St.
Manawa, WI 54949
(414) 596-2511
Products: Instant Nonfat Dry Milk,
Cocoa & Chocolate Products,
Powdered Drink Mixes, Non Dairy
Creamer, Iced Tea Mix & Instant
Tea, Orange Breakfast Drink

Sun Coast Plastics, Inc.
2202 Industrial Blvd.
Sarasota, FL 33580
(813) 355-7166
Products: Plastic Liners Closures

Sun Harbor Industries
2251 San Diego Ave. Suite A-216
San Diego, CA 92110
(714) 295-1221
Products: Canned Sardines, Canned
Tuna, Canned Mackerel, Canned
Cat Food, Canned Mandarin
Oranges, Canned Vegetables

Sunshine Chemical Corp.
60 Austin Blvd.
Commack, NY 11725
(516) 764-2800
Products: Liquid Dish Detergents,
Liquid Laundry Detergents, Powder
Laundry Detergents, Automatic
Dish Detergents, Fabric Softeners,
All Purpose Cleaners

Sunstar Foods, Inc.
757 Golden Valley Road
Golden Valley, MN 55427
(612) 546-2506
Products: Peanut Butter, Honey,
Pancake & Waffle Syrup, Potato
Chips

Superbowl Pet Foods, Inc.
P.O. Box 86
Maspeth, NY 11378
(212) 786-2468
Products: Dry Dog Food, Dry Cat
Food, Soft-Moist Dog Food, Soft-
Moist Cat Food

Superior Nut Co., Inc.
225 Monsignor O'Brien Highway
Cambridge, MA 02141
(617) 876-3808
Products: Misc. Candy, Misc. Dairy
Products, Dry Toasted Nuts, Misc.
Nuts, Salted Nuts, Chopped
Peanuts

Superpharm Corp.
155 Oval Drive
Central Islip, NY 11722
(516) 582-3223
Products: Over-the-Counter Drugs,
Proprietary Drugs

Suppositoria Labs., Inc.
135 Florida St.
Farmingdale, NY 11735
Products: Aspirin Suppositories,
Bisacodyl Suppositories,
Hemorrhoidal Suppositories

Swift & Co. (Grocery Div.)
115 W. Jackson Blvd.
Chicago, IL 60604
(312) 431-2000
Products: Canned Ration Dog
Food, Canned Chunky Dog Food,
Canned Ration Cat Food, Generic
Dog Food (Wet), Generic Cat Food
(Wet)

Synfleur
585 Winters Ave.
Paramus, NJ 07652
(201) 261-7601
Products: Flavorings, Perfumes

Technair Packaging Labs., Inc.
414 E. Inman Ave.
Rahway, NJ 07065
(201) 382-7270
Products: Window Cleaners, Liquid
Laundry Detergents,

Tee Pee Olives, Inc.
109 Montgomery Ave.
P.O. Box 239
Scarsdale, NY 10583
(914) 986-8816
Products: Green Olives, Ripe Olives

Tenco (Div. of Tetley, Inc.)
P.O. Box 15
Linden, NJ 07037
(201) 862-6600
Products: Soluble Coffee, Instant
Tea, Tea Bags, Flavored Drinks,
Decaffeinated Products, Lemon
Crystals

Tenco (Division of Tetley, Inc.)
Canal & Jefferson Sts.
Bristol, PA 19007
(215) 788-5546
Products: Tea Bags, Flavored Tea
Bags, Herbal Tea Bags,
Decaffeinated Tea Bags, Loose
Packaged Tea, Bulk Teas and
Spices

Tennessee Doughnut Corp.
2975 Armory Drive
P.O. Box 41004
Nashville, TN 37204
(615) 256-6500
Products: Frozen Glazed Donuts,
Frozen Cinnamon Buns, Frozen
Jelly Donuts, Frozen Honey Buns,
Frozen Sugar 'n' Spice Snacks

Texas Citrus Exchange
P.O. Box 793
Mission, TX 78572
(512) 585-8336
Products: Orange Juice, Grapefruit
Juice, Blended Orange/Grapefruit
Juice

Texas Farm Products Co.
P.O. Box 9
Nacogdoches, TX 75961
(713) 564-3711
Products: Pet Food, Fertilizer,
Lawn & Garden Chemicals, Feed

117

Thames Pharmacal
3 Fairchild Court
Plainview, NY 11803
(516) 349-8824
Products: Lotion, Hydrocortisone
Cream, Bacitracin Ointment, Triple
Antibiotic Ointment, Analgesic
Ointment, Jojoba Oil Shampoo

Thomas Farms
Swift Lake Drive
Shopton, NY 13435
Products: Jams, Jellies, Preserves

Thompson Industries, Inc.
2501 East Magnolia St.
Phoenix, AZ 85034
(602) 275-4711
Products: Styrofoam Cups

3 M
3M Center 223-25 E.
St. Paul, MN 55144
(612) 733-4565
Products: Private Label & Generic
Colof Slide & Print Film

Three P Products Corp.
5 Cooper St.
Burlington, NJ 08016
(609) 387-2240
Products: Generic Drugs, Over-the-
Counter Drugs, Vitamins,
Ointments & Creams, Dental Floss,
Thermometers

Time Chemical, Inc.
3870 Browns Mill Road, S.E.
Atlanta, GA 30354-9990
(404) 767-7526
Products: Dish Detergents, Laundry
Detergents, Cleanser

Tishcon Corp.
29 New York Ave. P.O. Box 331
Westbury, NY 11590
(516) 333-3050
Products: Vitamins & Food
Supplements, Over-the-Counter
Drugs, Timed Release Cold &
Cough Capsules, Timed Release
Diet aid Capsules

Toastmaster, Inc.
(Ingraham Products Div.)
Old Laurel Hill Church Road
P.O. Box 1609
Laurenburg, NC 28352
(919) 276-3101
Products: Clocks, Timers

Toliba Cheese, Inc.
45 E. Scott St.
Fond du Lac, WI 54935
(414) 921-3500
Products: Grated Parmesan &
Romano Cheeses, Shredded Pizza
Cheeses, Mozzarella, Blue Cheese,
Pizza Products, Misc. Cheeses

J.E. Toll Co.
76 Louise Drive
Ivyland, PA 18974
(201) 297-8520
Products: Bulk Extracts, Flavorings,
Perfumes

Tom's Foods
P.O. Box 60
Columbus, OH 31994
(404) 323-2721
Products: Candy, Potato Chips,
Nuts

Torbitt & Castleman Co.
Highway 146 P.O. Box 98
Buckner, KY 40010
(502) 222-1424
Products: Pancake & Waffle Syrup,
Barbeque Sauce, Chocolate Syrup

Treasure Isle, Inc.
P.O. Box 1126
Tampa, FL 33601
Products: Breaded Shrimp, Raw
Peeled Shrimp, Cooked Peeled
Shrimp, Seafood Specialties

Tree Ripe Products Co.
21 Sherwood Lane
Fairfield, NJ 07006
Products: Cocktail Mixes

118

Tuck Tape
Le Fevre Lane
New Rochelle, NY 10801
(914) 235-1000
Products: Cellophane Tape, Write-on Tape, Strapping Tape, Packing Tape

Tuckoff's Horseradish Products Co., Inc.
1101 South Conkling St.
Baltimore, MD 21224
(301) 327-6585; (800) 638-7343
Products: Horseradish, Mustard, Cocktail Sauce, Hot Sauce

Turf Cheesecake
158 South 12th Ave.
Mt. Vernon, NY 10550
(212) 654-1622
Products: Cheesecake

Twinoak Products, Inc.
R.R. 2 Box 56
Plano, IL 60545
(312) 552-7646
Products: Toilet Bowl Cleaner, All Purpose Cleaner, Bathroom Cleaner

Tyrrells, Inc.
115 N. 35th St. P.O. Box 31126
Seattle, WA 98103
(206) 632-4472
Products: Canned Dog Food, Canned Cat Food, Dry Dog Food, Dry Cat Food

U.S. Brands Corp.
P.O. Box 1997
Buffalo, NY 14219
(800) 828-7040
Products: Sugar Products

U.S. Products, Inc.
16636 N.W. 54th Ave.
Miami Lakes, FL 33014
Products: Vitamins, Private Formulations, Skin Care Products, Hair Care Products, Lotions, Pet Nutrients

Unelko Corp.
14425 N. 79th St.
Scottsdale, AZ 85260
(602) 991-7272
Products: Automotive Products

Uni Coop
Box CC
San Juan, Puerto Rico 00936
(809) 792-3000
Products: Oil, Corned Beef, Tomato Sauce, Juice & Nectars, Canned Vegetables, Rice

Union Carbide Corp.
Old Ridgebury Road
Danbury, CT 06817
(203) 794-3924; (203) 794-2000
Products: Plastic Wrap & Bags, Plastic Garbage Can Liners, Plastic Type Kitchen Wrap, Plastic Lawn Bags, Plastic Sandwich Food Bags, Plastic Trash Can Liners

Union Foods
320 Kalmus Drive
Costa Mesa, CA 92626
(714) 546-1962
Products: Ramen Noodles, Ramen Cups

Unisource Foods Corp.
2000 Division
Detroit, MI 48207
(313) 259-9410
Products: Cake Mixes, Frosting Mixes, Cookie Mixes, Gelatin Dessert, Doughnut Mixes

United Coatings, Inc.
3050 N. Rockwell
Chicago, IL 60618
(312) 583-3700
Products: Aerosol Paints, Paint Rollers, Paint Brushes, Latex Paints, Oil Paints, Solvents

United Foods, Inc.
(Western Operations)
P.O. Box 3111
Modesto, CA 95353
(209) 577-4477
Products: Broccoli, Brussel Sprouts,

Valvoline Oil Co.
P.O. Box 14000
Lexington, KY 40512
(606) 268-7487
Products: Motor Oil, Transmission
Fluid

Van Brode Industries, Inc.
56 Sterling St.
Clinton, MA 01510
(617) 365-4541
Products: Plastic Disposable
Cutlery, Plastic Disposable Plates
and Bowls, Handiwash Towlettes

Van Dutch Products Corp.
2417 Third Ave. P.O. Box 790
New York, NY 10451
(212) 292-0300
Products: Cocoa Mix, Instant
Chocolate Mixes, Cocoa, Puddings,
Gelatins, Iced Tea Mix

Velvet Food Products
30111 Schoolcraft
Livonia, MI 48150
(313) 937-0600
Products: Peanut Butter

Venice Maid Co.
P.O. Box 1505
Vineland, NJ 08360
(609) 691-2100
Products: Beef Ravioli, Spaghetti &
Meatballs, Corned Beef Hash, Beef
Stew, Dietetic Products, Pancake
Syrup

Ventre Packing Co., Inc.
373 Spencer St.
Syracuse, NY 13204
Products: Spaghetti Sauce, Catsup,
Mexican Sauces, Barbecue Sauces

Ventura Coastal Corporation
2325 Vista Del Mar
Ventura, CA 93001
(805) 653-7011
Products: Frozen Apple Juice,
Frozen Grape Juice, Lemon & Lime
Juice, Frozen Lemonade, Frozen
Orange Juice

Vi-Jon Laboratories, Inc.
6300 Etzel Ave.
St. Louis, MO 63133
(314) 721-2990
Products: Nail Polish Remover,
Mouthwash, Petroleum Jelly,
Hydrogen Perioxide, Isopropyl
Alcohol, Shampoo/Conditioners

Vince Farms, Inc.
13370 E. Firestone Blvd.
Santa Fe Springs, CA 90670
(213) 921-4494
Products: Frozen Crinkle Cut
Carrots, Frozen Baby Whole
Carrots, Frozen Stew Vegetables

Virginia Dare Extract Co., Inc.
882 Third Ave.
Brooklyn, NY 11232
(212) 778-1776
Products: Extracts, Syrups,
Cooking Wine

Vita-Fresh Vitamin Co., Inc.
7366 Orangewood Ave.
Garden Grove, CA 92641
(714) 898-9936
Products: Vitamins

The Vitarine Co., Inc.
227-15 No. Conduit Ave.
Springfield Gardens, NY 11413
(212) 276-8600
Products: Vitamins & Food
Supplements, Diet Aids, Laxatives,
Sleeping Aids

Vlasic Foods, Inc.
33200 West 14 Mile Road
West Bloomfield, MI 48033
(313) 851-9400
Products: Fresh Pack Pickles,
Processed Pickles, Relishes, Peppers

WCS Corporation
2498 American Ave.
Hayward, CA 94545
(415) 782-8727
Products: All Fabric Detergent
Booster Bleach, Room & Rug
Deodorizer, Automatic Dishwasher

United Foods, Inc.
(Frozen Food Div.)
P.O. Box 119
Bells, TN 38006
Products: Frozen Vegetables (Food
Service and Retail)

United Pacific Packers
500 Wall St. Suite 410
Seattle, WA 98121
(206) 622-1061
Products: Frozen Fruit Drinks,
Frozen Fruit, Frozen Misc. Juices,
Frozen Potatoes, Frozen Misc.
Vegetables

United States Testing, Inc.
1415 Park Ave.
Hoboken, NJ 07030
(201) 792-2400
Products: Product Performance
Testing, Advertising Claim Support,
Quality Assurance Services, Testing
Services, Environmental Testing
Services, Chemical Analysis

United Super Apparel
(The U.S.A. Co.)
815 Borad Ave.
Ridgefield, NJ 07656
(201) 943-4320
Products: Kitchen & Bath Towels,
Tablecovers, Pot Holders, Oven
Mitts, Wash Cloths, Rugs

Universal Label Co.
9895 Wayne Ave.
Cincinnati, OH 45215
(513) 554-0800
Products: Pressure Sensitive Labels,
Plain Paper Labels, Bar Soap
Bundling Tapes, Meat Label Inserts,
On-Pack Promotional Coupons

Vacu-Dry Co.
8105 Edgewater Drive Suite 226
Oakland, CA 94621
(415) 569-6414
Products: Breakfast Drink Mixes,
Lemonade Drink Mix

Wagner Juice Co.
1131 S. 55th St.
Cicero, IL 60650
(312) 656-2015
Products: Natural Juice (All
Flavors), Juice Drinks (All Flavors),
Flavored Drinks, Table Syrup,
Cooking & Salad Oil

Waldwick Plastics Corporation
21-23 Industrial Park
Waldwick, NJ 07463
(201) 444-7805
Products: Room Fresheners,
Household Toilet Products,
Insecticide Products

Walle Corp.
422 Natchez St.
New Orleans, LA 70130
(504) 831-0863
Products: Labels

Wampole, Inc.
180 Duncan Mill Road Suite 402
Don Mills, Ontario,
Canada M3B 1Z6
(416) 447-6408
Products: Cough Remedies, Internal
Analgesics, Vitamins & Food
Supplements

Warner-Jenkinson Co. of California
17500 Gillette Ave.
Irvine, CA 92714
(714) 557-7770
Products: Salad Dressing Mixes,
Lemon & Lime Juice, Party Dips,
Vanilla (Imitation & Pure)

Weber Food Products Co.
6710 E. Florence Ave.
Bell Gardens, CA 90201
(213) 773-3518
Products: Macaroni, Spaghetti, Egg
Noodles

Webster Industries, Inc.
58 Pulaski St. P.O. Box 3119
Peabody, MA 01960
(617) 532-2000
Products: Plastic Trash Bags,
Plastic Tall Kitchen Can Bags,
Plastic Sandwich Bags, Plastic Food
Storage Bags, Plastic Wrap, Plastic
Indoor Waste Bags

Weeks & Leo Co., Inc.
P.O. Box 3570
Des Moines, IA 50322
Products: Vitamins, Over-the-
Counter Drugs, Toiletries

The Weetabix Co., Inc.
20 Cameron St.
Clinton, MA 01510
(617) 368-0991
Products: Ready-to-Eat Cereals,
Cereal Bars

Weinad Biscuit Co., Inc.
(Sub. of Mazzola Biscuit Co., Inc.)
P.O. Box H Parksville Station
Brooklyn, NY 11204
Products: Crackers, Cookies,
Biscuits

Welton Associates, Inc.
2970 Peachtree Road, N.W.
Atlanta, GA 30305
(404) 237-0225
Products: Laundry Detergents,
Dishwasher Detergents

West Penn Oil, Inc.
1425 Market St.
Warren, PA
(814) 723-9000
Products: Dry Gas, Motor Oils,
Two Cycle Oils, Bar & Chain Oil,
Anti-Freeze, Charcoal Lighter

Westcan Pharmaceuticals
150 Beghin Ave.
Winnipeg, Manitoba, Canada
(204) 222-7389
Products: Vitamins, Food
Supplements, Over-the-Counter
Preparations, Health Food Products

The Western Food Products Co.,
Inc. (Sub. of Red Wing Co., Inc.)
P.O. Box 1524
Hutchinson, KS 67501
(316) 665-5541
Products: Jams and Jellies, Pickles
and Relishes, Tomato Products,
Vinegar, Syrup, Dressings

Western Garden Marketing
5410 S. Lake Shore Drive
Tempe, AZ 85283
(602) 839-0266
Products: Potting soil

Weyerhaeuser Co.
Tacoma, WA 98477
(206) 924-2604
Products: Disposable Diapers,
Sanitary Napkins, Diaper Doublers

Whink Products Co.
1901 15th Ave.
Eldora, IA 50627
(515) 858-3456
Products: Bubble Bath, Shampoo,
Rinse-Conditioner, Household
Cleaners, Disc Coffee Filters

White King, Inc.
P.O. Box 2198 Terminal Annex
Los Angeles, CA 90051
(213) 627-5011
Products: All Purpose Laundry
Detergent, Concentrated Low
Sudsing Detergent, Powdered Dry
Bleach, Bath & Complexion Bar
Soaps, Generic Detergents, Generic
Bar Soaps

White Rose Tea, Inc.
1501 Park Ave.
Linden, NJ 07036
(201) 925-8890
Products: Liquid Tea Concentrate,
Maple Syrup, Iced Tea Mix, Instant
Tea, Soft Drink Mixes, Instant
Coffee